HEEERE'S ED . . .
AND HERE'S YOUR
CHANCE TO MASTER
THE ART OF
PUBLIC SPEAKING

If public speaking is an art, then Ed McMahon is a Michelangelo—and he can help you make your speech a masterpiece. He draws on nearly three and a half decades of on-the-dais experience to offer a step-by-step guide to oratorical excellence.

Whatever your forum—whether it's onstage or offstage, at a PTA meeting or a board meeting—you'll discover how to deliver your speech with total self-assurance. You'll get laughs, you'll get applause, you'll get their attention. You'll make a speech you can be proud of—and you'll love every minute of it!

THE ART
OF PUBLIC
SPEAKING

Ed McMahon

BALLANTINE BOOKS • NEW YORK

Library of Congress Catalog Card Number: 85-25744

ISBN 0-345-34422-7

This edition published by arrangement with G.P. Putnam's Sons, a Division of The Putnam Publishing Group, Inc.

Manufactured in the United States of America

First Ballantine Books Edition: August 1987

AUTHOR'S NOTE

*My proceeds from this book
have been donated to
The Ed McMahon Scholarship Endowment
for the
Speech and Drama Department
of
The Catholic University of America
Washington, D.C.*

ACKNOWLEDGMENTS

No book is the product of one mind; every author blends his or her personal ideas and experiences with knowledge acquired from others. On this one, though, I've been helped by an unusually large number of people—everybody in any audience I've addressed has contributed to my development as a speaker. Wherever you are, I thank you.

More specifically, I must single out five people whose aid was essential in completing this manual. Lester Blank steered it safely around every shoal; Dr. Terrie G. Elliott generously shared her expertise as a public-speaking coach; Warren Jamison organized and edited my material; Madeline Kelly patiently read every revision; the late Bill Libby worked on the first draft.

—E. McM.

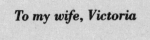

To my wife, Victoria

CONTENTS

FOREWORD

Thirty-odd years ago Ed and I were undergraduate students at The Catholic University of America. Then we took separate paths.

Ed achieved celebrity and fortune by what looked like serendipity but actually was an incredible amount of determination and hard work. I've followed an academic road —teaching, coaching and critiquing college students, then graduate students and others whose success in politics, business or the professions has intensified their need for greater speaking skills.

Ed has learned those skills by pushing the traditional methods of practicing, doing and studying to new heights. Few people have had his variety of on-the-job training for public speaking. Few have shared the spotlight with so many of this century's other stars and eminent people, thereby gaining the opportunity to observe what worked for them with audiences.

Before his teens Ed was practicing daily, using a flashlight for a mike. At fifteen he reached the doing stage, broadcasting as far as a sound truck's speakers could be heard. He's seldom been far from a mike since. A few years after he left college Ed had thirteen TV shows on the air in Philadelphia at the same time.

One reason for his popularity in those days was Ed's willingness to speak to local groups—after breakfast, lunch, dinner or whenever. If he could fit the occasion into his tight schedule—and somehow he usually could—he was there. It's an example we could all take to heart. Time *can* be found for public speaking, and it's a dynamic way to advance one's career and influence.

Now it's time for Ed to share what he's learned, not by teaching a small group but by reaching out to a larger audience—the readers of this book.

When Ed asked me to serve as his consultant I was flattered and excited. I still am. This guide is practical, focused, easy to follow, and it has a sound theoretical base. It's a serious manuscript with a light touch. It will help rank beginners, the kind I've so often seen with terror in their eyes at the prospect of speaking before a group. It will also help the more advanced speaker who has learned to hide the terror within.

However, merely reading this book will *not* make you a better speaker. *Doing it*—following the advice, practicing and striving for excellence, addressing audiences every chance you get—will.

Good luck,
Terrie G. Elliott, Ph.D.

PREFACE

While creating a speech you are at one with Michelangelo studying a raw block of Carrara marble. You and I would see only a squarish lump of white stone; the sculptor saw the magnificent statue concealed inside.

Michelangelo used sharp tools and faultless technique to release his masterpieces from the waste rock surrounding them. Yet the primary act of creation took place in his mind.

Like Michelangelo searching the mountains for Italy's finest marble, in preparing a speech you must pass over infinitely more material than you select. Like Michelangelo you must first create a masterpiece in your brain, because no one's delivered speech can be better than their conception of it. Like Michelangelo you must use tools to release your conception from what now obscures it—masses of extraneous information.

When your purpose is fully developed, how well you deliver your speech becomes all-important. Michelangelo was a designer without peer, but he would have achieved nothing had he not mastered the techniques of communicating his visions to his audiences.

This book first tells you how to cut away everything obscuring the fine speech that now exists only in your hopes.

In addition it tells you how to use the tools and techniques needed to rough out, carve and polish your creation.

And it also tells you how to please and inform your audience when you deliver your speech.

Do those three things and you will achieve your aims in giving speeches, whether those aims are to advance your career, to further causes you believe in, or simply to acquit yourself well.

CHAPTER 1

How to Turn Stage Fright into a Positive Force

Everybody expects the appointed person to face two things without fear—the dentist's drill and the microphone. The drill and the podium—when looking at either for the first time, one might feel the situations have a lot in common.

They don't. Giving a speech is not automatically as painful as keeping an appointment with your dentist.

That's cold comfort when you know the speech you're worried about giving can open great opportunities for you. It's no comfort at all if just the thought of facing an audience turns squirrels loose in your stomach.

If you exploit stage fright in a methodical way, you'll give a better speech. First understand that stage fright isn't something you'll ever get rid of completely. I haven't. Before every public appearance I feel the tension build; I have

1

a sense of growing concentration; I feel myself rising to the occasion. These are the hunter's emotions as he stalks his prey and at last moves in to drive his spear home. Forget about obliterating stage fright—your goal should be to help it give you greater awareness, higher concentration and a finer performance.

But that's not what you're worried about. Now is a good time to ask: Exactly what bothers you about getting up to give your next speech? Your feelings may come down to five clammy emotions:

- the fear of facing all those beady eyes;
- the fear that your message won't impress them;
- the fear that you'll mess up the delivery;
- the fear of giving an audience the right to judge you;
- the fear of showng fear.

Begin gaining control of beady-eye fear by convincing yourself the audience *wants you to succeed*. They really do. It's the only way they can feel good about taking the time and putting forth the effort to be there. So they are on your side when you stand up to inform and entertain them. They wish you well. They're eager to help you succeed.

But knowing the audience wants you to succeed isn't enough if you have a serious case of beady-eye fear. Reducing this fear to easily manageable proportions demands aggressive action, like joining groups in which everybody takes turns getting up to speak while all the others do the beady-eye bit.

A local meeting of Toastmasters International can be helpful in this regard. To locate a convenient Toastmasters meeting, call their headquarters in Santa Ana, California, at (714) 542-6793.

For conquering beady-eye fear the best situation is a small public-speaking training course where everybody sits with glazed eyes awaiting the dread call to stand up, march to the front of the classroom, and deliver their words. A pervasive, infectious fear hangs in the air like diesel fumes. It's the coldest audience you'll ever face, because those waiting their turn to speak are too nervous to understand a word you say, and those who have already given their short talks are too relieved to care. Only the instructor hears you.

Your first session will be the worst because the fear cracking through the air gets to you. But by continuing these sessions as frequently as possible, you'll experience a rapid decrease in fear. Keep telling yourself, "It isn't worth getting upset—nothing really happens." This is like the modern practice of applying cold instead of heat to athletic injuries—when the ice is removed blood rushes in and rapid healing takes place. Similarly, when you face your real audience, who are listeners instead of a tense group sweating out their own speeches, you'll be buoyed by the relaxed atmosphere.

What if you're scheduled to speak in a few days and don't have time for such a leisurely approach? Here are two quick fixes.

Quick fix number one. If you wanted to improve your golf or tennis game in a hurry, you'd go to a pro, right? And you'd expect one-on-one instruction, wouldn't you?

People often think public-speaking instruction only takes place in classes that run for a semester. However, you can get all the advantages of individual instruction from a public-speaking pro and speed your learning process enormously.

When you know you need a lot of help fast, read straight through this short book first. Get started on the preliminary work it suggests. Then locate a public-speaking pro who'll give you private sessions.

Quick fix number two. Take an orange crate to a busy downtown street where you're not known, get up on the crate and, using all your lung power, proceed to exhort the passersby with the speech you're preparing. I'm serious. This works because you can't continue feeling the really paralyzing fear of stage fright over and over—your nervous system rebels against going through all that turmoil for no reason.

Get rid of flop sweat in the anonymity of a public street or a city park's path where it doesn't matter. Repeat the street performance until you have your feelings under control. The alternative is to delay experiencing the worst moments of stage fright until you rise to give your speech, perhaps on an important occasion when the people you most want to impress are watching.

The second fear, that your message won't impress your listeners, is a necessary one. Use it to channel more and more energy into writing and polishing your speech until you *know* it will satisfy the audience.

Chapter 2 starts the process. Giving the right speech means you must first ask the right questions.

Chapter 3 provides a timesaving plan you can put to work right now to create the speech you want to give.

Chapter 4 is filled with tips on injecting humor into your remarks.

Some speakers lose the audience's initial goodwill after they've talked for a short time. Chapter 5 shows you how to avoid this catastrophe.

Chapter 6 tells you how to write a good, well-balanced speech.

Chapter 7 shows you how to take that good speech and turn it into a memorable one.

Coping with the third fear, that you'll mess up the delivery of your speech, is covered in Chapters 8 and 9. Here it's enough to say that a few slips of the lip don't matter. Even the most experienced speakers blow lines—it happens so often we've built a TV show around tangled tongues. Your bloopers are always good for a laugh, and in Chapter 9 I'll also give you a few ideas about carrying on after one of them.

And, in Chapter 10, I'll give you the full text of one of my speeches that incorporates many of the tips and techniques given in this book.

The fourth fear, of letting an audience judge you, is intensified at the podium because you're in a new situation. You can feel stage fright any time you put yourself in a new situation before other people. When I took my act to Las Vegas for the first time I had stage fright until I got my first laugh. After that I felt in sync with the audience and the remaining stage fright turned naturally into performing energy.

Don't try to deny, ignore or dull your mind to stage fright. It's raw energy, churning and straining to break free. Instead of hating and suffering with the dry mouth, the shakes and the butterflies, accept them. Visualize yourself converting those symptoms of raw energy into extra performing power. That's the key to using stage fright as a positive force—grab that energy and shove it right into your performance.

This leaves us with the last fear, that of allowing your stage fright to show. Trust me. This one will vanish of its own accord when you have the other fears under control. Beating stage fright comes down to having the desire and being prepared.

Some tricks help.

To ease tension, create familiarity. In the afternoon before the event go to the hall and examine the arrangements. Take your speech notes along. Find the exact spot you'll occupy while giving the speech and stand there for a few minutes looking over the room.

It's worth the effort to get the mike hooked up so you can test it out. Give some of your own speech, recite poetry—say whatever comes to mind. The idea is to hear your own voice in that hall and prove to yourself it doesn't hurt. When you return in the evening to give your speech you won't be a stranger, you'll be going back to a friendly place you know.

If you can, practice your entire speech on your afternoon visit. You don't need anybody's permission in an empty hall—just go ahead and do it. One woman received a rousing round of applause from the workmen setting up tables for the event. Since she was making her first speech to a large audience that evening, the practice run gave her a tremendous lift.

Check the lighting. There are two major concerns:

First, make sure you can read your notes easily at the podium. If you can't, getting a few hours' notice will provide ample time to solve the problem. Otherwise you won't make the exciting discovery that you'll be winging your speech without notes until you step up to address the audience.

Second, check whether there'll be a spotlight. When the house lights dim and the spotlight focuses on you, it's dramatic—you've automatically got everyone's attention. If you're not ready for that much limelight, make your feelings known to the stage electrician or program director. In any case, make sure the spotlight won't hit you with blinding force, making it impossible to see your notes, the audience, or much of anything.

Get comfortable with the precise location where you'll give your speech. Leaf all the way through your notes while standing there so you'll know exactly how you'll handle this small but important logistical detail. Little difficulties—like discovering you need two hands for your notes and one for the mike—can be disastrous last-minute surprises.

Then go through a litle psych-down. Put things in perspective—no after-dinner speech will stop the next morning's sun from rising.

If there's a podium, use it when you give your speech. Grab hold. Hit it to emphasize a point. Kick the thing to relieve tension.

If you're self-conscious about your notes, pick them up and shake them at the audience. Let them know you haven't memorized your remarks. You don't have to be perfect.

Just don't be dull. Prepare a speech that will keep the audience so entertained, involved, inspired or surprised that they don't have a chance to notice any tension you might feel. Do that and stage fright will remain only as a necessary—even welcome—stimulant.

Above all, enjoy giving your talk. With adequate preparation you're sure to do well, so have fun at the head table and at the podium.

· ·

Leave Out: "I forgot to say. . ." Just say it.

· ·

•••

Leave Out: "I don't know why I was picked to give this speech." Why tell the audience they're the victims of someone's bad judgment?

•••

CHAPTER 2

What to Ask Before You Agree to Speak

Question the person extending the invitation first. Then question yourself second. Finally, make the decision.

Avoid compressing this three-step process into the initial phone call. A hasty refusal may cut you off from wonderful opportunities; a hasty acceptance may involve you in a time-consuming project that can't be justified.

During the initial phone call, learn all you can about the occasion and what you should talk about, the group that will hear the speech, and the circumstances under which it will be given. Then insist on taking some time to make your decision.

"This sounds intriguing," you might say. "I'll check my schedule and get back to you by Thursday."

There's an exception. If your stomach knots up at the

9

mere suggestion of giving a speech, immediately refuse any invitation that doesn't allow you at least ninety days to prepare.

When program chairpeople need silver tongues on short notice, it's usually for reasons beyond their control. Nevertheless they should find practiced speakers rather than call on the unprepared.

If your rhetorical skills are undeveloped you must not only conceive, write, revise, rehearse and deliver your speech, you must first learn how to do all those things. This means your task in preparing to give a single speech is many times greater than that faced by a practiced speaker.

Allow yourself enough time to prepare and all will be well. Public speaking is the best—and often the only—key to many opportunities. If the speech you're being invited to give will be your first important one, be sure to give yourself every reasonable break. Your aim should be to make that speech the beginning of a new cycle of personal growth.

FOCAL POINT, MESSAGE, PURPOSE AND MOTIVATION

As you talk to the person inviting you to speak, start searching for answers to the four questions that follow. You don't have to arrive at your exact final response to each of them yet—just be aware of their importance to your decision. The questions are:

- What would the focal points of my speech be?
- What would my message be?

- What purposes would I hope to achieve by giving this speech?
- What's in it for me?

Put off deciding whether to give the speech until you can answer each of those questions in twenty words or less. If you can't boil each of your answers down to one short sentence, you haven't thought the matter through yet. Now let's define those four terms.

Your Focal Points

When someone wants you to speak at their parents' fiftieth wedding anniversary, your focal point has to be the happy couple's long and fruitful life. The focal point at graduations is the transition into adulthood; at awards dinners it's congratulating the winners.

At such rituals the occasion dictates the focal point, or points. You don't have any choice. Courtesy demands that your speech carry out the ceremony's aims, which comes down to meeting three requirements:

- to reward the audience's attention without overstaying your allotted time,
- to avoid belaboring your captive listeners with any personal convictions that aren't compatible with the occasion,
- and to speak cheerfully on happy occasions and seriously on somber ones.

The focal point is also clear if you're an expert on putting caps on bottles and the caller wants you to discuss recent developments in that field. Many times, however, the group inviting you has nothing specific in mind beyond wanting a good speaker for their next meeting. In these cases, it's up to you to find focal points that will interest most of your audience.

Here are examples of focal points:

For a welcome-back party. The focal points are the returning couple and their friends' joy at their return.

For a technical meeting. The focal points are the group's area of expertise (let's say, it's electrical engineering), and in your speech you will focus on two other points: how electrical power could be collected by satellites, and how it could be transmitted to earth.

Your Message

Compressing the essential point you want to make into a single sentence is a large step toward gaining a clear idea of exactly what you want to talk about and why.

For the welcome-back ceremony your message might be: The happy couple went through many trials without losing their devotion to each other or their determination to return to their wonderful hometown where you all live.

For the technical meeting it might be: Low-density microwave transmission of electrical power is feasible, safe and will eliminate the need for nuclear power plants on earth.

Your Purpose

Don't confuse what you want to achieve in giving the speech with your own motivation for doing so.

"What do I want the audience to do, feel or think as a

result of hearing my speech?" Your answer to that question is your purpose.

At the coming-back party, you want the returning couple to feel warmly welcomed and their friends to be happy they were part of it. At the technical meeting you want to awaken your listeners to space-age possibilities and obtain their support for the programs you believe in.

Your Motivation

We'll examine the fundamental issue of "What's in it for me?" later in this chapter when we look at the questions you should ask yourself.

QUESTIONS FOR THE INVITER

Begin by establishing where and when the speech is to be given and that you can be free at the right time. Then get into the arrival and departure questions. Is air travel involved? If so, will you be picked up at the airport or must you make your own arrangements for ground transportation and lodging?

When You'd Be Speaking at a Ceremony

At occasions where certain individuals or happenings are the focal point—awards banquets, roasts, victory celebrations, installation dinners and commemorative events of all kinds—a key concern is: How can I get all the background information on those people or happenings that I must have to create the right speech at this ceremony?

Don't agree to give the speech until you know how you

can get that information. Finding it may be harder than you bargained for, and once you agree to speak, the program chairman may feel it's entirely your problem.

The Audience

One of the first things the inviter will tell you is the expected size of the crowd. That's only the first thing you need to know about the audience. That group will assemble at a certain time and place for specific reasons. What are those reasons?

Often the interests, values and beliefs shared by the group are the forces drawing them together. Many times those forces will be family, friendship and occupation. The more you know about the common qualities running through your audience, the better your chances of succeeding with them.

People gather to express their various identities and reinforce their affiliations. Do you share any of their loyalties, interests and memories? The answer may be obvious. If it isn't, don't hesitate to ask.

Having little in common with the expected audience can be a disadvantage—unless you decide to treat that fact as an advantage. Many a compelling talk has been given by speakers playing off their differences from the audience.

Here are some more questions you might want to ask about the audience you're contemplating addressing:

- Will they know who I am?
- Will they be impressed by my credentials?
- How well informed are they likely to be about my topic?

- What age range, income range and educational level is most prevalent among them?
- Does the majority of the audience share the same occupation? Do they come from the same state or city?
- Are there any other background characteristics common to most of that audience?

The Speaking Environment

Learn all you can about the physical conditions under which you'll be speaking. Also find out whether the inviter and the sponsoring organization are experienced at putting on such affairs. If they're not, be on your guard. For example, the chairperson may assume the hall will provide a public-address system; the hall may assume the chairperson knows they won't. Mix-ups of this kind often reveal themselves when it's too late to correct them. Where does that leave you? With a bunch of unhappy people in the back yelling, "We can't hear."

If a public-address system will be required, someone in the inviting organization must take responsibility, not only for providing the sound hookup but also for making sure the system works well. You might be wise to find out who that person is before agreeing to speak.

Will the speech be given in a large auditorium or banquet hall? Or will a small room be used?

Will there be a lectern for your notes?

Will you stand on a stage to speak, sit on a high stool, or be seated behind a head table until you step up to the microphone?

If it's a small group will all of you—speakers and listeners alike—be seated around one large table?

The Program

How long a speech will you be expected to give?

Who will introduce you?

Will there be someone to signal you if you're running out of time?

Will there be more than one speaker? If so, will you be first, second, last? How long are other speakers apt to speak?

If you won't be first, who will you follow?

Will there be a question-and-answer period?

Will someone interrupt if the question-and-answer sessions runs too long? Or will it be your responsibility to stay within the schedule?

Does the organization have other business to conduct before or after your speech?

Do the members of the audience have other places they're scheduled to go that night?

QUESTIONS FOR YOURSELF

Before you agree to give a speech is the time to take a hard look at why you should do so. Having a strong internal purpose makes it an exciting challenge; lacking any firm purpose makes preparing for the speech an aggravating chore.

Start by asking yourself, "What's in it for me? In view of my other commitments, can I justify spending the time it'll take to prepare thoroughly?"

Because you'll be taking on a serious responsibility by agreeing to give a speech, these are fair questions.

16

A fair answer is that giving one speech probably won't make much difference in your life—unless it turns you on to public speaking.

The "Cross of Gold" speech that catapulted William Jennings Bryan from obscurity to a string of presidential nominations is often cited as a case where one speech revolutionized someone's life. However, Bryan was an accomplished speaker long before the first Democratic Convention that nominated him convened.

But you don't take up tennis to play one match. Being a frequent and effective public speaker offers great professional and personal benefits that can increase your satisfaction and income throughout your life.

So one of the best questions to ask yourself is, "Will giving this speech help me develop my speaking skills?"

Unless you already have a heavy speaking schedule, the answer to that one probably has to be yes if you see public speaking as an important element in reaching the success you want. This means that the opportunity to practice before a live audience is all the motivation you need.

THE DECISION

Giving speeches will widen your contacts, increase your influence and create opportunities to further your career. Speaking can also allow you to help advance the social, political and cultural causes you believe in. All these factors provide convincing answers to the question of what's in it for you.

I enjoy giving speeches. I can't think of a better reason for doing anything that's not illegal, immoral or fattening than for the simple enjoyment of doing it. You'll probably enjoy giving speeches too just as soon as you feel comfortable doing so. If that's your expectation, open yourself up to speaking opportunities.

Start slowly. Perfect your act in the smaller clubs before you take it to your personal Las Vegas. The first speech you're invited to give may have no influence at all on your career—but the next one might be crucial. Keep in mind that your second speech is sure to go better because of everything you learned giving the first. And the second dozen will go better than the first twelve.

The best idea is to look on public speaking as a skill that you'll never learn too much about or practice too often. This means you'll make it a habit. It also means you'll start collecting ideas and quotations for future use, and polishing bits of material before you actually need them. You'll start looking at the world with a sharper eye and listening with a keener ear. In the final analysis, public speaking is another way—one of the best—to expand your personal power and to live life more fully.

But, before you call back and say you'll do it on the particular invitation you're considering now, take a few minutes to jot down your answers to the four basic questions:

- What's my focal point for this speech?
- In one sentence, what will my message be?
- What purpose will I be trying to achieve in the listeners' minds?
- What's my personal payoff in agreeing to stand up and be heard?

18

Look at your answers. Do they satisfy you? If so, call back and say you'll do it.

Then turn to the next chapter and find out how to develop the best possible speech in the shortest possible time.

• •

Leave Out: "Unaccustomed as I am . . ."
The idea is to keep them from figuring that out.

• •

CHAPTER 3

Keys to Creating Better Speeches Faster

It's possible to be both brief and boring but it isn't easy— brevity and boredom are natural enemies. On the other hand, tedium and long-windedness love each other. The phrase "a long, boring speech" is a cliché. If you told someone, "I heard a *short*, boring speech last night," you'd probably get an odd look.

Not that it's easier to give a brief speech than a long-winded one. Woodrow Wilson once apologized for writing a long letter, saying that if he'd had more time he would have written a shorter one.

What do you tell an audience when you drone on and on? That you don't think their collective time is worth much. Otherwise you would have invested enough of your individual time to hone your speech into a brisk and interesting presentation.

20

In an effective short speech the speaker weaves a tight web of ideas into the allotted time. When the speech is given, those ideas sail out over the audience like a net—and you've got them.

TAKING AIM

Aim your mind at creating a speech you'll be glad you gave.

To do that effectively, go to a private place with an hour or two and a means of capturing your thoughts. A pencil works fine—you may prefer to use a marker pen and board, a tape recorder or dictating machine, a typewriter or word processor.

Take one other thing along: the answers to the questions at the end of Chapter 2. Those answers are like a flight plan for your speech. Whenever you're working on it, keep your flight plan in sight to remind you to keep heading in the right direction.

During your aiming session, explore two things: *what you need* in the way of delivery training, and *what your speech needs* in the way of research and study. Then work out a schedule for getting what's needed.

Later chapters go into delivery training. Study the Thousand-Seconds Plan and the Who-Did-What-to-Whom Approach in this chapter to zero in quickly on what your speech needs.

THE THOUSAND-SECONDS PLAN

When is the last time you heard a speech that was too short?

The ideal after-dinner speech lasts 1,000 seconds—that is, 16⅔ minutes. Notice that I didn't say, ". . . lasts about a quarter of an hour." Minutes are loose, hours are sloppy. When you're thinking seconds, you're thinking lean. Think lean from the beginning and you'll talk lean—you'll grab the audience's attention and hold it because your speech will be packed solid with things they want to hear.

At first glance you might suppose that filling a thousand seconds with attention-holding words requires an enormous amount of effort. One thousand can be a daunting number. It won't look so tough when you break it down into small units you can work with easily:

	Seconds Used
Opening remarks	100
Body of the speech:	
5 sections averaging 170 seconds each	850
Closing remarks	50
Total	1,000

Your speech will probably break down somewhat differently—you may need 150 seconds for your opening remarks and 100 seconds for your summary. This still leaves 750 seconds for the body, which should be divided into five sections that average 150 seconds in length.

Bear in mind that these sections don't necessarily coincide with the main points you plan to make in your speech. A good speech has between two and five main points. If you have only two, you might cover the first main point in sections 1 and 2 and the second main point in sections 3, 4 and 5.

Why five sections? For two reasons. First, it greatly simplifies revision and rehearsal. Second, if you have to cut your speech short at the last minute, you merely cut entire sections.

The idea is to start strong and finish even stronger. Begin by catching their interest fast; leave them with something good at the end. This means your most important material should be in the fifth section, and your second most important material should be in the first section.

If you go to the podium under time pressure, you know exactly how you can shorten your remarks and still give an effective speech. If you have time for two sections, deliver section 1 and then say something like: "Time doesn't permit me to give you all the information I've prepared. I'll move right to the main point I want to make today."

And now you launch into section 5, which you've already determined is your most important argument. If you don't even have time for section 1, you can still jump right to section 5 with the same introductory paragraph that's quoted above.

In order to insure this kind of flexibility and control, lay out the body of your speech in terms of five short sections from the beginning. However, don't press too hard to make the sections exactly equal in length—it's far more important to cut unneeded details and concentrate on the most important material. The body of your speech might shape up like this:

Section 1	70 seconds
Section 2	120 seconds
Section 3	220 seconds

Section 4	170 seconds
Section 5	270 seconds
Total	850 seconds

If the body of your speech needs 850 seconds, you're left with only 150 seconds to get on and off. This means your favorite shaggy dog story is out; open with a few one-liners instead.

Although it's much too early for final decisions on exactly how your speech will break down, impose time discipline on yourself from the beginning. All the way through its composition, revision, rehearsal and delivery keep your plan firmly in mind: opening remarks, 100 seconds; five short sections averaging 170 seconds; closing remarks, 50 seconds; total, 1,000 seconds. If any area runs longer, some other area has to be cut a corresponding amount.

Is there anything sacred about the 1,000 seconds? Certainly not. Unless you're the featured speaker of the evening, feel free to speak for 500 seconds—or just 150 if you prefer. However, unless you're an experienced speaker *and* the occasion *demands* a longer address—a rare event in after-dinner speeches—don't consider imposing a longer speech on an audience.

This brings us to a vital point: How many words are involved in a speech that takes a given length of time to deliver?

CONVERTING SECONDS INTO WORDS

Most experienced public speakers talk at the rate of about 150 words per minute because they get their best response at that speed. That's 2½ words per second, which means you'll need around 2,500 words for your 1,000-second address.

In Chapter 6 we'll take up the question of whether you should write your speech word for word. If you were to do so in manuscript form, your 2,500 words would require about a dozen pages of double-spaced typing on on 8½ x 11-inch paper. With adequate margins all around, a sheet of letter-sized paper accommodates 24 lines of about 9 words each, or about 216 words per page.

GETTING STARTED

Begin by listing all the subtopics that might be adequate for one of the five sections. If you'll let your speech grow over a period of days, being careful to work on it regularly so it remains bright in your mind, you'll soon discover that you have a lot more than five possible subtopics. That's good.

Jot down your ideas for the speech as they occur to you while you're going about your usual activities. When you sit down for your daily half hour with the speech, you'll have new material to work with.

Keep fitting your ideas into the five sections in outline form, discarding the irrelevant observations, the weak arguments, the unnecessary details. In this way concepts that looked good at first will be supplanted by even better concepts. The exact composition and sequence of the five sections may change several times—a sign that you're developing a much stronger speech than your first outline indicated.

If you don't find the subtopics coming to mind easily, try the interrogatory approach. While you're communing with yourself in private, imagine that you're a member of the audience you're planning to address. What will they want to know about your subject?

THE WHO-DID-WHAT-TO-WHOM? APPROACH

A strong speech tells the audience what they want to know just as they are forming questions in their minds.

It doesn't happen by accident. Neither is it difficult. Let's say the subject of your speech is pollution in a nearby river. Sit down for a hard-think session and write questions as fast as you can come up with them. Your first list might look like this:

How bad is the pollution?
Aren't the upstream mines to blame?
How about pesticide and fertilizer runoff from farms?
And what about the chemical plants on the river?
What damage is the pollution doing to plants and
    wildlife?
How dangerous is it to people?
What can be done about it?
Is it increasing or decreasing?
How much will cleaning up the pollution cost?
Who's going to pay for it?

When you run out of questions, put your first list of them aside for a day to freshen your outlook. You may find that writing that first list will point out areas in which your knowledge of the subject is incomplete or in need of updating. You may think of organizations to call, people to interview, sites to visit.

As you research your subject, keep working your list of questions over. Add promising new ideas. Regardless of how much time you've put into developing them, ruthlessly cut any points you realize your speech doesn't need to communicate its message and advance your purposes in giving it.

Also rearrange the questions in the order that you'll discuss them. While you're reorganizing the sequence, list all the important subtopics that you'll need to cover under one of the primary questions. Do that and you have outlined your speech.

Your list of questions, now revised into an outline, might turn out like this:

Section

1. What kind of pollution are we talking about?
    How dangerous is it—
        —to people?
        —to plants and wildlife?
    Is the pollution increasing or decreasing?

2. What benefits will we gain by cleaning up the river?
    Priceless gains—
        —health
        —quality of life
        —ecology
    Economic gains—
        —increased tourism
        —higher property values

3. Who and what is causing the pollution?
    Local fertilizer runoff
    Local chemical plants
    Mines upstream

4. How much will controlling pollution cost?
  Who's going to pay for it?
  Will the area lose jobs if we crack down on the
    polluters?

5. How can we clean up our river?
  Political action
  Legal remedies
  Volunteer vigilance essential

That's the outline of your speech. Now you're ready to consider humor, keeping the audience on your side and the other steps to giving a speech the audience will applaud.

THE LIGHTHEARTED SPEECH

Even the most lighthearted speech has a message, which comes down to something like this:

"For a few minutes tonight we're going to put our concerns and divisions aside and strengthen our common bonds by laughing together."

That's a good message, one I'm proud to have brought in person to many audiences. Naturally, I don't state the message in those words. Instead, I put that message across by wrapping it around the focal point of the occasion.

ONE NAIL AT A TIME

Build a speech like a carpenter builds a stairway, one nail at a time. Leaving out a step or two doesn't necessarily mean the stairway will fall apart—but it certainly makes climbing it a riskier proposition.

THE ART OF PUBLIC SPEAKING

Since all of us have a busy schedule, finding the time to prepare thoroughly isn't easy. Some important preparatory work can be done during odd moments, but unless you're an experienced public speaker, don't rely entirely on such a haphazard method.

Begin immediately to give your speech time on a regularly scheduled basis. This means putting off some other things until after you step down from the rostrum.

Untrained speakers sometimes do nothing about a speech until panic sets in a few days before the scheduled event. Then only three options remain:

- They can back out, at the cost of damaging their reputation and self-esteem.
- They can wing it, which invites disaster and maximizes stage fright.
- They can shove all other commitments aside and put every possible moment into preparing their speeches. This is doing it the hard way because this option doesn't allow enough elapsed time for change, growth and learning to take place.

I've been describing a better way, a way that makes a much smaller demand on your nerves and time, a way that insures the best performance possible. This way can be summed up in seven words: *Work at it a little every day.* Here is this approach in detail:

1. The best time to start putting ideas for your next speech down on paper is while you're accepting the invitation to speak. You can't start too soon. The longer your mind works on the speech, the better it'll be.

2. Without fail, give a little of your prime time every day to working on your speech. Just thirty minutes a day—at an hour when you're at your peak level of alertness and creativity—are enough to keep your speech growing in depth of concept and richness of expression. Get up half an hour early if you have to—but get those thirty minutes a day in. When you face your audience, you'll be thankful you did.

3. Take your speech notes and a pad of blank paper wherever you go so you can use odd moments to work on perfecting your speech.

Sometimes I scribble notes for my speeches on any handy scrap of paper, often at the last minute. However, this isn't a practice I recommend to the inexperienced. Until you've gained self-confidence on the rostrum, prepare for your appearances by carrying a small notebook or packet of cards so you'll be able to record the gems of thought that come unexpectedly.

I can be more casual about speech preparation because my primary activity for many years has been appearing before audiences. Over that period I've had to develop a vast amount of material I can deliver without additional preparation.

I never give the same speech twice. What I say turns mostly on the occasion, on who's there, on the interests of the audience and on what's happening in the world that week. Mingled with the new elements are stories, facts and ideas from my inventory of prepared material. In both experience and preparation, almost my entire life has been a rehearsal for the next speech I'll give.

Your next after-dinner speech will also reflect your entire life. When you stop to think about it, you have a huge reservoir of experience and knowledge to draw on in preparing your remarks. However, unless you too have a vast amount of material rehearsed and ready, you'll be in the awkward position of trying to fly on one wing. You should invest the time and energy that preparing thoroughly demands.

* *

> *Leave Out: generalizations and abstractions.*
> **If your mind wanders, so will the audience's.**

* *

CHAPTER 4

How to Get Laughs from the Head Table

The oldest opening line in speechmaking is, "A funny thing happened to me on the way here tonight." There are good reasons for this line's continuing popularity, and in a few seconds I'll tell you how to brighten it with fresh twists.

An unusual occurrence—something you can shape into a funny story—can always happen while you're on your way to give a speech. In fact, it's more likely to happen at this time because you're in a heightened state of awareness.

So be flexible. Be willing to change your opener. But don't depend on finding a joke at the last minute that you can use.

In theory, the oldest line allows you to tie in a joke that

really has nothing to do with the occasion. In practice, it's hard to get a laugh this way. Ideally your opening joke not only ties in with you, the occasion and the audience, it also ties in with your message. Such a grand slam of relevancy is sure to be a big hit, the bad news is it's almost impossible to find such a joke. Tying in with yourself is easy. Find a way to hit one more point of relevancy—place, audience or message. Then you'll wring smiles from blank faces, make the smilers chuckle, raise chuckles to laughs, and turn laughs into sidesplitters.

This effect works faster in reverse. Take a joke that's a sidesplitter because it advances your message, ties in with the audience or is relevant to the occasion. Tell the same story when it clearly has no connection with your message, the audience or the occasion, and you're likely to hear your watch tick in the dead silence that follows. All those blank faces are not a pretty sight.

However, it's easier to get the second laugh than the first. If your occasion-fitting material is a little wobbly, maybe you need some hilarious stories to lead the way—but are they hilarious the way you tell them?

Find out when it won't hurt too much to fall flat. If you won't have any opportunity to try your material out before your next after-dinner speech, skip the irrelevant jokes. No speech was ever helped by attempts at humor that flopped.

Using the oldest opening line in its original form might make the audience wonder if they've also heard the joke you're about to tell. To avoid putting that thought in their heads, freshen your opener with a twist or two. Joe Cook showed the way years ago by starting his after-dinner speeches with:

"I've been coming to affairs like this all my life. Every

time I do, some guy gets up and says, 'A funny thing happened to me on the way here tonight.'

"And, you know," Cook would continue, "in all these years nothing funny ever happened to *me* on the way to one of these things."

Cook would get a small laugh with that one and then a big one by adding, "Until tonight." In those days his audiences hadn't heard that twist.

Nowadays you're likely to hear Joe Cook's twist almost every time the oldest opening line is used. Audiences expect it. If they've already had a lot of laughs, it can still get a chuckle. But if it's been a pretty serious meeting up to then you need a new twist:

". . . nothing funny ever happened to *me* on the way to one of these things." No pause. *"Not* even *tonight."*

Now you pause, but not too long. The audience may be too confused at this point to chuckle. But they're getting ready—they're hoping—they're primed.

Now hit them with, "But it *did* happen to me last week when I was . . ." and now you tie your joke to the audience, the locality or the message. You can pull in almost any joke with variations on that phrase.

It's a good way to begin a speech. However, I must tell you that I don't use this opener.

I like to start with a geographical tie-in. Speaking in a new conference center near an old hotel, I said:

"I feel something very comfortable about being here. I don't know what it is, but maybe it's being across the street from the Pickwill Hotel.

"I remember hearing that my mother and father were traveling in this area before I was born, and they must have stayed at that hotel. As a matter of fact, I found an old Bible. In the front of the Bible there were some notations of great things my mother experienced.

"Let's see now, it was June 6th, 1922. That's right, it was June 6, 1922."

(You see how I've got them? Hold their interest by moving along quickly—that is, by not piling on too many details. But you still have to take it a step at a time.)

"And in the Bible it said, 'Pickwill Hotel, Buffalo, New York, weekend with my husband. Greatest night of my life.'"

Then I went on with, "I don't know why that's stuck in my mind, but I feel so comfortable here. June 6th. Golly, that was nine months before I was born!"

The whole place dies. You were conceived across the street from where you're speaking!

That's a true story, Bible entry and all. I used it one night in Buffalo, New York.

BUILD LAUGHS AROUND THE SIX ASPECTS OF RELEVANCY

When you're standing before an audience with a mike in your hand, there are six separate areas of relevancy you can talk about. Any one area will sustain a joke by itself, but with a little ingenuity you can weave a second or even a third relevancy into your jest, thus making it even more funny. The six areas of relevancy are:

- *You*, your interests, cultural background, hopes, fears and history; your family, friends and enemies; anything that touches you or the people you know in imagination or reality.
- *The audience*, their educational, religious, cultural

or ethnic background; their interests or occupations; anything else that concerns them or that they interact with.

- *The location,* which can be the room, building, city, state or region where you're speaking.
- *The occasion,* the organization staging it and anything related to its past, present or future; the people who are active in or friendly to the organization; the people and organizations that aren't friendly to your audience.
- *Your message,* especially anything that shows an unexpected facet of it.
- *The news,* world, national or local.

That's a lot of relevancy.

Audiences don't have to have to study humor to know there are plenty of things you can joke about that will interest them, so they're instinctivly impatient if they can't see how a joke relates to them, to today or to the business at hand. It's hard enough to get a laugh with relevant material; don't multiply your problems by a factor of ten by trying to use irrelevant jokes.

Let's look at a typical example of an irrelevant joke as an opener. The president of a national professional association recently began his address to a prestigious group of civic leaders in this manner:

Coming to this microphone, standing in the shadows of so many illustrious speakers who have preceded me, and facing this impressive group of distinguished people is a rare privilege.

It's a once-in-a-lifetime experience that brings to mind two baseball fans who spent most of their lives together. They played on the same team in high school, college and semipro. As they grew older, they played on the same neighborhood softball team. They knew every obscure statistic of every major league player. Baseball consumed most of their waking hours. Late in life they began musing about heaven and wondered, "Is there baseball in heaven?"

They made a pact. The first to die would come back and tell the other. In time Bob died. Days, weeks and months went by with no word, although Jack always ended his evening prayers by saying, "Bob, if you're out there, please tell me, is there baseball in heaven?"

Just as he was about to fall asleep one night a voice called, "Jack, this is Bob. I have great news—there *is* baseball in heaven."

"Is that right?" Jack asked.

"Absolutely," the voice said. "You're pitching Tuesday."

So here I am pitching to you. Between us, you and I share some awesome responsibilities . . .

Some of the audience responded with a forced chuckle, most remained silent. Clearly, the audience felt the irrelevant joke was patronizing. The speaker had no connection with baseball; his subject had no connection with baseball; the audience had no connection with baseball. Why then did the speaker use a baseball joke?

He wanted to be able to say, "So here I am pitching to you." For that he dropped a deadly old joke on the crowd, making it clear at the beginning that he could give the same speech in any state without changing a word.

And all the time he had a great opening line, one that, although lacking in humor, would immediatley compliment his listeners rather than patronize them. That line was, "Between us, you and I share some awesome responsibilities . . ."

WORKING UP JOKES

Jokes often depend on an offhand manner that masks careful wording and timing. The listeners must get the point—but tell too much and nobody laughs. There's a sharp line between funny and unfunny, one that even professional comedians can't always predict. That's why they like to perfect their material in the smaller clubs before hitting the big time with it.

I suggest sitting down with your jokes and working out their essentials. Think about the timing and the key words. Then write them out and get the essential elements firmly in mind.

However, you have to be careful not to sound as though you've memorized the joke or story—unless your delivery is like that of a certain stand-up comic on one of the TV programs I emcee. After his act, I described him on the show as having a "kick it along the street and don't give a damn" style. Solemn manner, wooden delivery and all, he was still very funny.

Try your jokes out on a one-to-one basis or with small groups before you use them at the podium. I like to try jokes out several times on different people to get the wording and timing just right.

Keep looking for relevancy. Memorize the six points of relevancy we discussed a few paragraphs back, and use them to rule out any joke that doesn't qualify on at least one point. Better yet, try for at least two points of relevancy on every joke you use at the podium. Never forget that the better the joke fits the occasion, the funnier the audience will think it is.

"If that's true," you may ask, "why is it that a stand-up

comedian can get laughs with off-the-wall stuff that has absolutely nothing to do with the audience or the occasion?"

Look closer and you'll see that the comedian is usually hitting on at least two of the six points of relevancy with all his or her material. Much stand-up comedy bounces off the comic's family, friends and personal experiences. And, since the audience knows their message is "Laugh at this," any zaniness is accepted as relevant. They hit the third point of relevancy by playing off current events or the daily problems we all face. Three out of six isn't bad—and that's without hitting on an easy one, jokes and one-liners about the locality where they're performing.

If your speech has any purpose other than to get laughs, you don't have to tell a single joke or whip off even one one-liner. If you're convinced you can't pull humor off, don't attempt it. Too many speakers stand up and grimly get what they think is the obligatory joke out of the way. In the serious speech humor is never obligatory.

A funny story that fits the occasion or an amusing anecdote usually works better for the average speaker than a joke will. When a story works, it relaxes the audience, making for a warm and receptive attitude.

You can often brighten your presentation simply by taking a lighthearted look at your subject or at yourself. It's always safer to poke fun at yourself than at someone else. If you are well known for something and willing to poke fun at yourself about it, it's usually good for a laugh that'll loosen the audience up.

George Allen, the football coach, had incurred the sportswriters' wrath for not letting his players drink water during hot preseason practice sessions. Later he turned that into a surefire laugh at his banquet speeches by opening with, "Does everyone have their glass of water?"

Under similar circumstances Don Shula, one of the most celebrated coaches in the history of professional football, used a story about taking his wife on vacation to a small seaside town in Maine. He'd heard it was a quiet place where they could relax without anyone paying attention to them.

It was raining when they arrived and there wasn't much to do. Seeing a small theater, they decided to take in a movie. When they entered the lights were on and the show hadn't started. To their surprise a scattered handful of people gave them a nice litle round of applause as they seated themselves.

Secretly pleased, Shula whispered to his wife, "I guess there isn't anywhere I'm not known."

"You're known and loved the world over," she replied with a touch of sarcasm.

A man came over with a friendly smile on his face and they shook hands. Shula said, "I'm really surprised you know me here."

The man said, "Should I know you? We're just happy to see you folks—the manager said he wouldn't start the film until at least ten people came in."

THE ADVANCE TECHNIQUE

One of the best jobs of advance work ever done for me was turned in by my son, Mike, when I was preparing to deliver a speech at his school. Unless you're a politician, you don't need to hire an advance man. A friend can get you the information you need; often you can get it yourself over the phone.

What you're looking for are the names, nicknames and idiosyncrasies of people in the audience who are well known in that group.

Bob Hope brought this technique to perfection on his tours of armed forces bases. His advance people would find some of the commanding officer's quirks and some peculiarities about the local area. When Hope put those things into his monologue, the soldiers, sailors or marines roared with laughter.

But none of the stories or one-liners, no matter how funny on an Army base in Korea, for example, could be used on a show given on the deck of an aircraft carrier in the Mediterranean. The best and most dependable humor for an after-dinner audience is what they instantly know is aimed at them and them only.

ILLUSTRATING POINTS

A preacher is addressing a group at the rescue mission on the evils of drink. He has two glasses in front of him, one filled with water and the other with whiskey. The preacher takes out a plastic bag containing two worms.

"Watch this," he says as he drops one worm into the glass of water. The worm swims around, drinks deeply, gargles, and gets to where he's having a very good time doing the backstroke.

The preacher then drops the other worm into the glass of whiskey. The worm drinks deeply and suddenly sinks to the bottom, stone dead.

Leaning toward an obvious drunk in the front row, the preacher asks, "Does this teach you anything, my good man?"

The drunk admits, "It certainly does."

"And what is that?" asks the preacher triumphantly.

"It teaches me," says the drunk, "that if I keep on drinking whiskey, I'll never have worms."

The moral is: If you use a story to illustrate a point, make sure you think its implications through. The listeners may see it from a completely different viewpoint than you intend, with disastous results.

USING ONE-LINERS

The great monologuists roll them off one after another, making it look easy. It isn't. Keeping the laughs going not only takes good material that's current and relevant to the place and audience, it also demands a keen sense of timing. Without all those things, you'll feel like you're dying up there.

It goes better to slip the one-liners in here and there. When humor comes unexpectedly the laughs are longer and louder. You haven't nailed yourself to the wall with a "Hey, I'm going to tell a joke now" warning.

For example, if the subject of debate comes naturally into your speech, you can shoot in, "A lot of good arguments are spoiled by some fool who knows what he's talking about."

FINDING HUMOR YOU CAN USE

If you don't have the knack of creating your own humor, all is not lost. Bookstores have joke books that are arranged by subject. The problem is that much of this material gets out of date rather quickly.

The solution is to subscribe to a humor newsletter. The best I know is *Orben's Current Comedy*. (See the Sources appendix.)

. . . .

Leave Out: "*I don't want to offend anyone, but . . .*"
If that lead-in seems necessary, what you say
next will certainly offend somebody. It
might offend everybody.

. . . .

● ●

Leave Out: words you had to look up in the dictionary.
Nobody in the audience will bring one along.

● ●

CHAPTER 5

How to Keep the Audience on Your Side

Almost all after-dinner audiences are completely on your side when you stand up to speak. Even when you're speaking to people who are under an unusual strain or who have recently suffered reverses or a grievous personal loss, they want you to succeed.

They may hope to learn something from you; they may hope for laughter and a brief release from their cares; they may simply expect to hear some pertinent words. In any case, your success means they were right in coming to hear you. In this chapter I'll talk about five basic ways to keep the audience on your side.

TAKE CHARGE OF GETTING YOURSELF INTRODUCED RIGHT

In most cases your introducers are like your parents—you meet them on arrival. However, you don't have to trust entirely to luck for a good introduction; whoever draws that assignment will almost certainly welcome your help in preparing their remarks.

If things are left to chance, your introducer may make misleading statements you can't ignore, statements that are embarrassing and time-consuming to correct. Make sure your introducer has accurate, up-to-date information. However, it's not enough simply to hand the introducer a copy of your résumé. One speaker who did that listened with mounting chagrin while the entire résumé, including her home phone number, was read to the audience.

So keep in mind that whoever introduces you may be coming off a busy week or feeling a little stage fright. If that's the case, whatever you put in his hand is likely to be the introduction the audience will hear. And even if the introduction will be handled by a practiced speaker, your suggestions for it will probably be used, at least in part.

This means you should write an introduction that covers everything you want the audience to know about you. Writing in the third person ("he pioneered . . ." or "she is the president of . . .") allows you to list your accomplishments without sounding like you're bragging. Be brisk, be brief, but don't be boring.

Write your introduction out word for word; handing an outline to an introducer invites disaster. Try your first draft out on friends or associates and encourage suggestions.

When you're satisfied, type your introduction in CAPS, with each sentence starting at the left margin.

Copy shops are everywhere. Mail one copy to the introducer about ten days before the event. Bring another copy along when you meet him or her for breakfast on the big day. Have a third copy tucked in your notes when you appear at the banquet that evening.

Why three copies? The person originally scheduled to introduce you may come down with the flu. His replacement may meet you for breakfast and then forget to bring his copy of the introduction to the dinner.

It's your speech. Take responsibility for getting it launched right.

BE MERCIFUL WHEN THE HOUR IS LATE

When the hour hand is pointed toward the stars, your best move is to be brief. Don't try to make up for lost time by talking rapidly—tired audiences and superfast speeches don't mix.

When you go on late, skip the windup and the follow-through. This feels like chopping off your arm when you have carefully prepared your speech, but it must be done. Cut everything except a shortened statement of your main point. When you've said that, sit down.

I've never seen this handled better than at a recent West Coast affair. The program was running hours late when the featured speaker finally reached the mike. Perhaps half the audience would've felt cheated if he hadn't said anything; the other half just wanted to go home. He broke up that tense, late-night situation with, "Even in Tokyo it's one o'clock in the morning! I'm going to be brief." He kept his promise and the crowd was soon happily headed home.

You can't turn back the clock, and nothing good comes of trying, as one of our former presidents proved. It happened on one of my favorite occasions, the Football Hall of Fame dinner in New York. Each year they induct outstanding professional players as well as college men who have achieved greatness both on the gridiron and in their studies. An All-Conference tackle from the Southwest will stand up who's also getting a 3.9 grade point average in chemical engineering.

Cardinal Spellman might give the invocation. One night Senator John F. Kennedy was there to get the gold medal for his love of football. Lots of people must be recognized and heard from, so things can easily go into overtime.

Not until that fatal hour for speakers, one in the morning, was Herbert Hoover—then many years out of the White House—introduced to make the principal address. By that time people were falling asleep or sliding under the table. Ignoring the clock, Hoover delivered the same speech at 1 A.M. that he would have given at 9 P.M.

Before Hoover finished, two-thirds of the audience had vanished. Some staggered off to bed, others retreated to the nearest bar, no longer able to silently listen to the front table. Those who remained, it's safe to say, retained little of what Hoover said.

If you get on that late, you have no more than three minutes of the audience's full attention. Like it or not, your only play is to send them home quickly.

GET IT ACROSS FAST THAT YOU'RE WORTH LISTENING TO

To keep the audience on your side, show them you deserve their gift to you—a sizable chunk of their precious time. How can you do that? By shoveling the loose gravel off your ideas before you get there. By digging your boulder-sized ideas out of the ground before you get there. By crushing those huge rocks and extracting the essence of your message before you get there. And then after you get there, by giving them only the glittering gold that remains after all your careful processing.

To illustrate, let's look at two examples. In the first the speaker begins:

> Ladies and gentlemen: I don't have much to say today and I hope I don't bore you. As you know, I've been busy. In fact, I've just been too darn busy to put together the speech I'd really like to give here today, but I'll sure do the best I can.
>
> It was some time back, almost a hundred years ago, I guess—more than eighty years ago, anyway—I remember my grandmother told me about it. Maybe your grandmother told you about it too. Or your grandfather. We've all heard about it.
>
> The thing is, some of our ancestors, people that you either knew about or heard your parents or your grandparents talk about, had, well, an idea that we could form some sort of an association here in this land of theirs—and ours. You could call it a new country. And the idea of this new country was to be that, well, everybody, no matter who they were or who their parents were, or where they came from, or what they did, would be the same, or about the same in everything,

and would be free to do anything they wanted to do.

Now we find ourselves fighting among ourselves—father against son, brother against brother, family against family—over that idea.

Sound familiar? Our fictional speaker has already rambled on nearly as long as Abraham Lincoln took to deliver his entire Gettysburg Address more than a century ago:

Fourscore and seven years ago our fathers brought forth on this continent a new nation conceived in liberty and dedicated to the proposition that all men are created equal.

Now we are engaged in a great civil war, testing whether that nation, or any nation so conceived and so dedicated, can long endure. We are met on a great battlefield of that war.

We have come to dedicate a portion of that field as a final resting place for those who here gave their lives that that nation might live. It is altogether fitting and proper that we should do this.

But, in a larger sense, we can not dedicate, we can not consecrate, we can not hallow this ground. The brave men, living and dead, who struggled here have consecrated it far above our poor power to add or detract. The world will little note nor long remember what we say here, but it can never forget what they did here. It is for us the living, rather, to be dedicated to the unfinished work which they who fought here have thus far so nobly advanced. It is rather for us to be here dedicated to the great task remaining before us—that from these honored dead we take increased devotion to that cause for which they gave the last full measure of devotion—that we here highly resolve that these dead shall not have died in vain, that this nation, under God, shall have a new birth of freedom, and that government of the people, by the people, for the people, shall not perish from the earth.

Those two hundred fifty words are considered by many to be the finest speech ever delivered by an American. Edward Everett, the principal speaker that day at Gettysburg, wrote Lincoln a few days later, "I should be glad if I could flatter myself that I came as near the central idea of the occasion in two hours as you did in two minutes."

Except on solemn occasions, most audiences today expect to be entertained as well as informed. Even so, you and I can learn much about economy of words, vivid expression and compelling cadence from Lincoln's short, eloquent address.

CONVINCE THE AUDIENCE THAT YOU KNOW THEM

Whether your purpose is to entertain or inform, the audience needs to be convinced that you know where you are and who they are. They want to know that you cared enough to bring the best—a message that relates directly to their interests, their concerns, their dreams. This is a must, this adaptation to the social context.

For this reason, no two speeches should ever be identical, particularly in their beginnings. Use your opening remarks to grab the audience's attention by making them feel special.

Show them you're not just trying to be entertaining, you're trying to tie your words in to them. Even though I'm an entertainer and I've reached a certain level of celebrity by working so long in this business, I work at finding common ground with all my after-dinner audiences.

Since I consider myself to be first, last and always a

salesman, I use that fact. Everybody sells, whether it's directly, in the form of marketing products and services, or less obviously, as in persuading people to accept their ideas, leadership or beliefs.

Many of my audiences are in sales of some sort, which makes it easy for me to tie in. It may take some study, but you have many things in common with the audience you'll soon address. Find those shared values, qualities and backgrounds; then use those points of contact to put yourself on an equal basis with them. Finding and using that common core between you and your audience is what makes for speaking success.

To a religious audience I would say, "As a young man, I too entertained the idea of becoming a priest. Unfortunately I did not fulfill that dream as you folks here tonight have."

Right away there's a great empathy between me and an audience of priests because I thought about becoming one. So tie that in.

Speaking to a group of politicians I'd say, "I almost had a life in politics. As a matter of fact I did have a political career—I was the mayor of Lowell, Massachusetts—for one Wednesday when I was twelve years old." You get a little laugh. You're talking to government people and you were in government for one day.

Always relate something from you to your audience. It bonds you together and puts you on the same plane as equals so you're not talking down to them or up to them— you're talking as one of them.

Adlai Stevenson could be the all-time champion of geographical tie-ins. Stevenson was a gifted speaker and might have been president had he not been matched against a great war hero, Dwight Eisenhower, soon after a popular war. On the campaign trail, Stevenson always found a truthful and interesting way at the beginning of his speech to connect himself to the locality where he was speaking. Here are a few of the ties he fashioned:

In Michigan: ". . . glad to be here in Grand Rapids on this Labor Day holiday. As a boy I spent my holidays in Northern Michigan."

In any farming state: "I own farmland in Illinois and come from a family that has lived in the heart of the corn belt for over a hundred years."

Anywhere in New England, another place where he had no real tie at all: "I don't know why it is that an American, no matter where he was born or where he lives, has a feeling in New England of coming home."

In Virginia he had to reach back three generations to find a geographic tie: "My grandfather, then a candidate for vice-president, spoke here in Richmond exactly sixty years ago this week."

In Kentucky he went back five generations: "I do not feel at all like a stranger in Kentucky. My great-great-grandparents were married here . . ."

Anyone who has at least one grandparent born in this country can probably connect with many localities in similar ways by shaking the family tree a little. Let's look at how other eminent people have tied themselves to their audiences geographically.

David Rockefeller in Forth Worth under the auspices of the Sid W. Richardson Foundation:

Thank you so much, Sid, for that warm and generous introduction. Visiting Texas always has been an enormous pleasure for me . . .

I have always felt very much at home in Texas, and, during some thirty trips here over the past thirty-four years, I have consistently carried away with me far more in the way of insights and knowledge than I have left behind. There are many reasons for this, but perhaps the most important is the renewed sense I have found on each visit of vision, energy, and the ability to think big.

Texans, of course, are world-renowned for thinking big, and I thus am especially pleased to be here once again to discuss a subject which I am convinced demands big thinking—private giving in America.

Lee A. Iacocca, the Chrysler Corporation's chairman of the board, at a meeting of the Poor Richard's Club in Philadelphia:

> . . . I'm also glad to be back in Philadelphia, so close to my roots. I spent a lot of my early years here, and I actually learned to love this city.
> . . . Of all the people in history, Ben Franklin is the man I'd most like to meet. I'd like to have a drink with him. (I'd have a scotch, and he'd have his glass of port.)
> He'd probably start by saying, "Iacocca, that's a hell of a name . . ."

Thomas P. O'Neill, Jr., Speaker of the House of Representatives, at the Alfred M. Landon Lecture on Public Issues, Kansas State University:

> Forty-nine years ago, the name of Governor Alf Landon appeared on the ballot as the Republican candidate for president of the United States. In the Commonwealth of Massachusetts, there appeared on some of the same ballots the name of a young Democratic candidate for State Legislature—Tip O'Neill.

That was my first successful campaign for public office. And I appreciate the opportunity to come out here today, to the home state of Alf Landon, to honor the man who headed the other political team back in 1936.

When you don't have tie of your own, come up with a graceful way to borrow someone else's, as Margaret Thatcher did when addressing a Joint Session of the United States Congress:

My thoughts turn to three earlier occasions when a British Prime Minister—Winston Churchill—has been honored by a call to address both Houses.

Among his many remarkable gifts Winston held a special advantage here—through his American mother he had ties of blood with you. Alas for me, these are not matters we can readily arrange for ourselves.

Those three occasions deserve to be recalled because they. . .

STOP DECISIVELY

Your close shouldn't come on slowly, like reluctant spring after a long, hard winter. Neither should it strike so suddenly the audience isn't sure you're finished until they see you sit down.

To keep the audience on your side, end with a snap that leaves them wanting more. But first let them know you're concluding. Say something like, "I'd like to leave you with this thought." Then live up to your promise—give them only one parting thought before you nod, step back and leave the podium.

It's either that snappy finish or else they're sitting there hoping only for the moment when you finally close your mouth for good.

· ·

**Leave Out: *apologies for being a bad speaker.*
They might not think you're bad unless you
insist on it.**

· ·

CHAPTER 6

Writing Your Speech Versus Speaking Your Speech

Writing a speech word for word is the traditional method. There's a better system. The new way is faster, easier and results in superior performances. Except for momentous speeches, the new way will always be better if you're able to take advantage of it.

Before you decide the occasion for your next after-dinner speech is indeed momentous and opt for the writing approach, hear me out.

It's not just that the language of speaking and writing each have their own peculiarities, problems and powers— the two modes of communication are different media. If you doubt it, read a play the night before you see it performed in a theater. Shakespeare is great for this but any good drama will do. Reading the play leaves you feeling you understand it all—until you *hear* as well as see it performed. Then you realize what a skeleton the printed form of dialogue and declamation is.

With every line the actors speak, unsuspected nuances come flooding at you. The fictional characters become real people as you hear their emotions expressed with swift changes in pitch, loudness and speed. Gestures speak volumes. Facial expressions reveal surprising depths of feeling. Pauses add drama. Even the actors' postures convey meaning. The play vibrates with life.

The successful speech also vibrates with life. By conveying a wealth of humanness, intensity and emotion it compels attention. To accomplish this you must rely on the arts of spoken language; at the podium the arts of written language are out of their element.

Writing your speech word for word means that at some later time you must translate it from the written language to the spoken language. This breathing of life into your transcript's inert pages is another step, a far more pressing and difficult one than many inexperienced speakers realize. It's a step that often becomes a formidable barrier between you and the audience—and between you and the success you want to achieve with your speech. This will certainly happen if you avoid translating your speech into spoken language until the moment you put your head down and start reading to the audience.

Operating on advanced levels, practiced orators leap over this barrier easily. Those less skilled often expect that reading their speech will provide a refuge from stage fright —instead they experience the full force of that fear. There are clear reasons for this effect.

Speechreaders isolate themselves from the audience.

Eye contact is infrequent and jarring instead of being nearly constant and reassuring. Having plenty of time to think about their nervousness (because merely reading aloud from a typed script doesn't fully occupy their attention) speechreaders are keenly aware of the crowd's dismay at being read to. This invariably causes them to hurry through their text, sacrificing the audience's comfort and comprehension in their fear-driven rush to be done.

Contrast this with delivering a speech from an outline. Since your mind is fully occupied with what you're saying, you don't have much time for stage fright. What little you do have quickly gets shoved right into your performance— as we discussed in Chapter 1. You're compelling because you're fully joined with the audience. As you talk your eyes are gathering information from their faces about whether you should speed up or slow down, skip an explanation or reemphasize a point, pause for effect or get on with it.

Right from the start, I recommend that you develop your speech primarily via spoken language. In other words, prepare your speech by talking it instead of writing it. Here's how to do that expeditiously.

WRITING A SPEECH WITH YOUR MOUTH

After carrying your speech through the steps called for in Chapters 2 and 3, you came away with a written outline of your speech. By *outline* I mean no more than two pages of short phrases written large.

Speechwriting with your mouth is the process of perfecting your remarks by using a tape recorder and your outline. Whenever you see a way to improve your outline you rewrite it; whenever you see a way to improve your speech, you re*speak* it.

Using your outline, stand your speech up. That is, deliver it to a tape recorder in an empty room. This is your first run-through.

Don't strain for memorable phrases yet. If they come to you, wonderful—jot them down in your notes. At this stage aim for a simple, clear and brisk expression of your ideas. Add the polish later.

Expect to make several false starts on your first run-through, and on subsequent run-throughs too. Don't worry about them. Just rewind the tape and begin again every time you exhaust your ideas, tangle your tongue or wander from your subject.

Remember, you're now working only on the body of your speech—no opening jokes or introductory remarks, no summary or other concluding statements. Get the main course cooking before you worry about the appetizer and dessert.

Talk with one eye on the clock. Don't let yourself talk longer than 850 seconds, which is the maximum time you're allowing for the body of the speech. At 850 seconds, stop and make a note of where you are on your outline. There are only three possibilities, and we'll discuss them in turn.

Short

You were all through before 500 seconds had elapsed. Ask yourself why.

Have I selected a subject that's complex enough for a fifteen-minute talk? If the subject is all right, am I generalizing too much?

Do I need more support material? More stories? More examples?

Or do I simply need more research and study?

Figure out what's wrong. Then get to work on the remedy.

Long

The clock ran out before you got past your outline's midpoint. Ask yourself: Am I covering too much ground? Is my purpose too broad? Am I getting bogged down in detail?

The quickest way to shorten a speech is to avoid entire areas. Wanting his inaugural speech to be brief, President-elect John F. Kennedy told his speechwriter, Theodore C. Sorensen, "Let's drop out the domestic stuff altogether." By thus limiting himself to foreign policy he was about to deliver a short address—it lasted about twelve minutes— that inspired the nation. Including domestic issues would have required at least twice as much time. "I don't want people to think I'm a windbag," Kennedy told Sorensen.

To keep your remarks short you too will have to avoid some important and interesting areas. (If one of them is so exciting, make it your main topic.) But either cover a sub-topic adequately or say nothing about it. Let the time limit guide you; accept its discipline; make the decisions it requires.

About right

At this stage of your preparation, you want your run-through to last between 750 and 1,000 seconds. Continue retalking your speech and revising your outline until it fits within those limits.

If additional research and study are required, reaching this about-right stage of initial preparation may take several sessions spread out over several days.

When you can run through your embryonic speech within the time limits, you're ready to move to the next step. Unles you're working with a speechwriter (other than yourself) move directly to Chapter 7 and start infusing your remarks with punch, pith and polish.

WORKING WITH A SPEECHWRITER EFFECTIVELY

"What do *I* want to say about this subject?" is a natural point for speakers to jump off from.

"What will that *particular* audience want to hear?" is often the approach a speechwriter thinks of right away.

I have a special feeling for speechwriters, having once worked as one. Before my overseas tour during the Korean conflict, I was the public information officer for the 3rd Marine Air Wing in Miami. The commanding general had me write his speeches to civilians defending our Korean involvement. He never bothered to give me his views nor allowed me to hear the speeches he delivered from my scripts. Before shipping out to Korea I wrote several of them; apparently I guessed right about what he wanted to say because the general didn't complain. And there you have a short case history of how *not* to work with a speechwriter.

Without direction, the speechwriter's difficulties multiply and your chances of getting a strong speech fade. All the occupants of the Oval Office have found time for regular meetings with their speechwriters, which undercuts anyone else's claim of being too busy.

Don't use a speechwriter who doesn't want to hear you give the speech or whom you don't want to take along. There are two reasons why the speechwriter should be there when you speak.

First, when you give the speech you'll be too preoccupied to retain much understanding of what worked and what didn't. With the speechwriter sitting in the audience, you have the best possible person monitoring the audience's reactions. By noting what you do best and what you should avoid, and by noticing the lines that struck home and those that missed the target, your speechwriter gains an enormous fund of information that will go into improving your next performance.

Second, late-breaking developments can outdate your speech a few hours before it's to be given. You may learn that your material has been, or will be, preempted by an earlier speaker. The event's excitement may spark new ideas for your speech. But if you're a busy participant you'll have little time to revise your speech by yourself.

How can you be sure a speechwriter's creation will sound like your own words? A good question—and one that has an easy solution.

While the speech is being developed over the course of several meetings, occasionally have the speechwriter give you not only the latest draft but also an outline. Then, working only from the outline, record the speech. Give that tape to the speechwriter, who can then incorporate your way of expressing yourself and more of your ideas into subsequent drafts.

In Washington, D.C., many speechwriters have been and are highly respected and well paid—and others continue to search for that happy circumstance. Often they must switch from boss to boss as people come and go in the seats of power.

These anonymous toilers aren't always given the opportunity to discuss the matter with their employer before the speech is due. They might have to work from position papers only, or complete the assignment with even less input from on high.

An assignment for an important speech on South American policy was given a writer by a high-flying politician who never bothered to talk to his speechwriter or even read his speeches before delivering them. All the writer heard from the pol's staff was that the address would be given before an influential group in New York.

The speech began by discussing several of the previous administration's failures. After each failure was scornfully described, the politician read a line promising a solution later in his speech. At last he approached the climax with these words:

"So I propose a ten-point plan for improving our relations with and position in South America. Here are the ten points."

The politician turned the page. It held only a brief personal message from his speechwriter:

"I quit, you SOB! Think up your own ten points."

When you work with a speechwriter, make the time to do it right. You won't be sorry you did.

• •

Leave Out: "I'm not a male (female) chauvinist, but..."
They'll decide what they think you are.

• •

CHAPTER 7

How to Infuse Your Speech with Punch and Polish: Make It Pithy

Once you have a rough draft of your speech taped, you're ready to add punch, polish and pith. *Webster's Ninth New Collegiate Dictionary* defines *pithy* in the sense I'm using as "having substance and point: tersely cogent" and in a cross-reference says, "*Pithy* adds to *succinct* or *terse* the implication of richness of meaning or substance."

Isn't that what the audience will be hoping for when they settle down to listen to you?

What makes a speech good? Dr. Terrie Elliott, an old friend from Catholic University and for many years a sought-after consultant in Washington, D.C., on public speaking, says:

"A good speaker speaks with me, not at me. His or her speech grabs my attention immediately and holds my attention throughout. It's well-organized. It touches me with personal elements. It's in tune with the social climate in which it is given. The speaker has something to say and says it, using stories and examples to bring the points made to life. Yet the speech doesn't try to cover too much and it ends a bit too soon, leaving me wishing I could hear more."

Many stirring speeches can be traced to genius or inspiration. If you're like me, you've given up on genius and can't afford to wait for inspiration. But you and I can knuckle down to work.

You may be like me in another respect—you can't spare large chunks of time for speech preparation. You don't have to. The best speeches I've given have been developed a little at a time over a period of weeks.

There are doubled values in working on a speech for at least a few minutes every day. First, there's the steady progress you'll make. Far more important is the effect of keeping your speech in the front of your mind—by doing so you'll grow special antennae that constantly search for facts, ideas, examples and humorous material to enliven and enrich your talk.

An effective speech has one central message. Enhance that message by adding stronger examples and more vivid expressions. Make room for them by discarding the less powerful passages and trimming unnecessary words. The aim always is to bring the audience forward to a more complete understanding and enjoyment of what you're saying. Everything that doesn't advance your purpose in making the speech must be chopped.

Be ruthless. Cut everything that doesn't entertain or inform your audience. The concept is simple—it's the execution that gets complicated.

If you're making the speech to inform them, get to the point fast—tell them what you're going to tell them.

If you're there to entertain them, get right into your first funny story. Just tell it. Skip the part about how you happened to hear that funny story—unless you can turn that tale into another funny story.

Getting to the meat of your message fast tells the audience two vital things—you know what you're doing, and unless they pay attention right now they'll miss some good stuff.

Later in this chapter I'll tell you how to grab and hold the audience's attention. However you can't stand up there hurling thunderbolts at them; a speech tightly packed with wide-ranging arguments and mind-boggling data leaves the audience floundering. But you must move along. You can't explain too much. You can't dawdle.

Support your ideas with facts and examples. Illustrate them with stories, which can be funny or emotional as long as they're apt.

REARRANGE YOUR SCHEDULE

During the period when you're perfecting your speech, rearrange your schedule so that you'll be meeting with and eating with the most interesting people you know. Whenever you can, guide your conversations with knowledgeable people toward the subjects you're going to talk about in your speech. Don't hesitate to whip out a pad and jot down any ideas that come up during these stimulating lunches and dinners. It's a real compliment to anyone that you want to preserve and use some of their ideas.

WORKING WITH THOSE WEAK EARS

The human race has always learned more through their eyes than their ears. Research indicates that audiences only hear about half of what the speakers say. How much do they remember the next day? The same research indicates it's less than a fourth of what little they did hear. How much do they remember after thirty days? A year? Don't ask.

Responsibility for this falls more on the speakers than on their audiences. Speakers do best when they communicate warm emotions rather than cold facts. If you move someone's feelings about your subject in the direction you desire, you've been far more persuasive than if they remember your saying that the per capita income in Qatar is $29,000, in Sri Lanka only $400.

THE AUDIENCE STANDS IN A FLOWING STREAM

Never forget that. With the printed page the reader can go back over anything not understood at first glance. Not so with the spoken words—the listener has only the first hearing to catch your meaning or it's gone. As a speaker your choice of words, of speaking pace and style, of example and arrangement is far more critical than when you write.

The best learning situations allow us to acquire information with both our eyes and ears, which is why audiovisual methods of teaching and selling are so effective and popular. To the banquet speaker, however, this is largely an academic matter. Visual aids—films, charts and the like —generally aren't appropriate for after-dinner speeches. Usually the banquet orator's bag of tricks includes only three visual effects: *facial expressions* and *gestures*, both covered in Chapter 8; and *spotlight*, mentioned in Chapter 1. All three are merely accessories—the success of your speech rides on how well the audience comprehends your words.

When you spring a surprise, you can pause for the moment it takes to sink in. Eye contact will tell you whether you must amplify or repeat your surprising statement. But for the most part your words must roll on and on, with new ideas coming fast.

CREATE A STRONG STRUCTURE FOR YOUR IDEAS

During Black History Month at Johns Hopkins University, Harry M. Singleton, assistant secretary for civil rights in the Department of Education during President Reagan's second administration, told the students:

> I was especially pleased at your invitation to speak today because it gives me a rare opportunity to share my thoughts on how we young, gifted and black must respond to the challenge of being rungs—for our children, for the young generation of potential achievers and for each other.
> I have secured for my own two little children five pearls of wisdom—five "heirlooms"— which I would like to share with you. They may sound archaic but they are words of advice whose value lies in the fact that

they reflect the vision and the strength of preceding generations, and have been tested and proved solid.
  —Take responsibility.
  —Work up to your capacity.
  —Embrace the American achievement ethic.
  —Dream the American Dream.
  —Color yourselves successful.

After setting forth that strong structure in his opening remarks, Mr. Singleton then elaborated on each of his five pearls of wisdom in the body of his speech. At the close he said: "In conclusion, I challenge you to also accept the five heirlooms," and then repeated them. Four more inspirational sentences brought this powerful speech to an end.

What made it powerful? Two things: the force of Mr. Singleton's reasoning and the strong structure he built his ideas on. Without the structure, his reasoning could not have been communicated so effectively.

USE POINTERS

Some years ago when Arthur Hughes was active on the banquet circuit, we appeared on programs together from time to time. On one occasion I complimented him on his speech.

Art chewed on his cigar and said, "You know what I do? I tell 'em what I'm going to tell 'em, I tell 'em, and then I tell 'em what I told them. When I've done that I sit down. Nothing to it."

Because we find it so difficult to grasp things that we hear, the speaker has to keep his speech organized so that all the way through he's pointing out ways for the audience to understand what he's saying.

In other words, keep telling people where you're taking them.

"We have two options in this community crisis that, unfortunately, not all of us fully appreciate.

"*One*, we can continue to muddle through, hoping for the best. However, the trend is clear. Two years from now...

"*Two*, we can accept reality and..."

Another pointer I use is, "Now that we've looked at (I name the topics I've been talking about), let us now examine____." This announces that a new subject will be discussed and provides a smooth transition to it. The new subject may be the solution to the problems mentioned earlier, or a somewhat contrasting subject.

PREPARING A CRUCIAL SPEECH

Suppose you're scheduled to give a speech that could have an important effect on your career. You are determined to do well and have plenty of time to prepare.

Such was the case before John F. Kennedy gave his inaugural address. The actual speechwriter was Theodore C. Sorensen, who in his book, *Kennedy*, states that "... pages, paragraphs and complete drafts had poured in...

"The final text included several phrases, sentences and themes suggested by these sources...

"But however numerous the assistant artisans, the principal architect of the Inaugural Address was John Fitzgerald Kennedy. Many of its most memorable passages can be traced to earlier Kennedy speeches and writings. For example:

Inaugural Address

For man holds in his mortal hands the power to abolish all forms of human poverty and all forms of human life.

... the torch has been passed to a new generation of Americans ...

And so, my fellow Americans, ask not what your country can do for you; ask what you can do for your country.

Other Addresses

... man ... has taken into his mortal hands the power to exterminate the entire species some seven times over.

It is time, in short, for a new generation of Americans.

We do not campaign stressing what our country is going to do for us as a people. We stress what we can do for the country, all of us."

Sorensen continues, "Each paragraph was reworded, reworked and reduced. The following table illustrates the attention paid to detailed changes:

First Draft

And if the fruits of cooperation prove sweeter than the dregs of suspicion, let both sides join ultimately in creating a true world order —neither a Pax Americana, nor a Pax Russiana, nor even a balance of power— but a community of power.

Next-to-Last Draft

And if a beachhead of cooperation can be made in the jungles of suspicion, let both sides join some day in creating, not a new balance of power but a new world of law ...

Final Text

And if a beachhead of cooperation
can push back the jungle of suspicion,
let both sides join in creating a new
endeavor, not a new balance of
power, but a new world of law..."

I've quoted only the last of four examples given in the book showing how the President-elect and Sorensen polished the first draft of Kennedy's Inaugural Address. With each revision they added punch, polish and pith.

The full text of Kennedy's Inaugural Address is given in Sorensen's book. It's only 1,900 words, well under the 2,500 I recommend as a top limit for after-dinner speeches. Kennedy spoke for only about thirteen minutes on that memorable occasion.

Before you decide to polish a speech in this manner, consider that it demands skills of a high order and consumes large amounts of time.

Don't invest that time unless you're certain you can deliver the resulting speech with verve and vigor instead of head-down speed. You'll be well-advised not to take the difficulty of doing so lightly—John F. Kennedy required a great deal of coaching and months of practice before he could read a speech in a convincing and forceful manner.

LEAVE OUT—

As the tape plays the latest run-through of your speech, listen for the following style problems. If you hear any, get rid of them before they lay a smoke screen between you and your audience.

Leave Out Superfluous Words That Aren't Needed

Omit the last three words in the above sentence and you have the same meaning. Better yet, leave out the third word—*superfluous*. The same number of syllables are dropped and you'll be more readily understood.

In every case, your speech will be stronger if you use the term on the right than if you cloud the issue with the phrase on the left:

in the event that	if
at this point in time	now
in the order of magnitude of	about
had the opportunity to be	was
come into possession of	get

Leave Out Redundancies

Some people aren't satisfied to call something a *part* or a *component*; it has to be a *component part*. A blizzard is always an icy blizzard or even a snowy blizzard. The same people never talk about a *disaster*—it's a *terrible disaster*, apparently to distinguish it from a *wonderful disaster*. And they never wait for *developments*, preferring to wait for *future developments*.

You don't have to spell it out in detail, give ample advance warnings and conceptualize future plans.

Just spell it out, give warning and make plans.

Leave Out Unnecessary Intensifiers

Is a *very big dog* larger than a *big dog*? If so, how much bigger? Nobody knows. *Very* is rarely needed.

Major, *absolutely* and *completely* are a few of the words used as unnecessary intensifiers. Take them out of the following and does the meaning change?

> a major turning point
> an absolutely essential move
> a completely defunct company

Leave Out Tired Terms

Phrases like *slow but sure*, *good as gold*, *right as rain*, and *hard as a rock* will paint old gray over your bright new ideas.

Leave Out Strings of Long Words

Since the oratorical infliction of polysyllabic configurations of labyrinthine construction inhibits, to an extraordinary degree, adequate comprehension by anyone whose aural sensitivity, present subject interest and/or language-sophistication level is at a substantial disadvantage when compared to the levels evidenced by the majority of the group, the inevitable result of employing such lengthy polysyllabic constructions must be that a proportion of the audience—probably if not certainly a significant proportion—will find the constructions incomprehensible, or at least not worth the effort that deciphering them would necessitate, thus creating feelings of dissatisfaction and restlessness in that disadvantaged segment of the audience which we can confidently predict will have the effect of distracting those who would otherwise be able to apprehend the speaker's most abstruse conceptualizations without undue difficulty.

All that says is: *Stringing long words together makes some of the audience restless, which distracts the others.*

Everything else in the preceding paragraph is gobbledygook. There a simple but worthwhile idea was expanded tenfold into a single sentence that by itself is half as long as Lincoln's Gettysburg Address.

If you find yourself stringing long words together, force yourself to state the same ideas in short, simple words. Doing that is like going into the steam room at the gym—you can't hide anything.

When you strip your ideas down to short simplicity, what remains? Your fresh and original thinking. Don't hide your brilliance under a bushel of bombast. Talk in simple terms. Use the time saved to cover more ground, to introduce new arguments and examples, to humanize and personalize your proposals, and to present your thoughts in a more powerful form. In the following sections we'll look at some ways to do that.

USE WORDS PEOPLE DON'T HAVE TO THINK ABOUT

In a speech, always use words people don't have to stop and think about. Your rhetoric must always be clear-cut words that people understand. A lot of speakers try to impress the audience with long words, but that backfires. You lose them. Getting into the big multisyllabic words that many people don't know the meaning of is really an admission that you don't know how to communicate.

If you're talking about the company's new sales campaign for the fall, it's a lot better to say, "We've got a solid team and everything's going for us. Now we're going to step up to the plate and hit a bunch of home runs. We're not only going to win the game, we're going to win the pennant." Everybody understands. They don't have to mull it over—the meaning is ingrained in their minds.

But if instead they hear, "We have an unparalleled opportunity in the upcoming season. The ramifications are awesome. If we realign our priorities and seize this opportunity without delay, victory will unquestionably be ours because . . ." They never hear the *because* 'cause you've already lost them.

Everyone should be with you all the way. In speechmaking you should always make sure of that. If you leave people wondering, "What does that mean?" pretty soon you're on point 5 and they're still back there puzzling over point 2 or point 3. That's one large reason why the researchers keep coming up with such dismal reports about how much listeners hear and retain.

Use phrases that paint pictures in the minds of the audience so they know what you're talking about. You can do it with taste. You can do it with sights. You can do it with sounds. Use all the senses. Make comparisons. "I'll tell you what it was as good as—a hot dog at the ballpark." Everyone knows exactly what that is. It's clear in everyone's mind. It touches everybody and makes your point instantly.

How can you paint mental pictures of sounds? Thunder in a canyon. Surf that crashed like Oahu's North Shore. As quiet as a kitten's step.

Appeal to the senses and paint images for the audience. That'll keep them even with you and eager to hear more. That's how you take your speech off your notes and put it in their laps.

VERBAL DEVICES

Lincoln's Gettysburg Address appears in its entirety in Chapter 5—ancient words in this age of rapid change. Yet they have the ring of today. You can do far worse than to begin each speech *perfecting* session by rereading that short, memorable address.

Three Is More Than Four

To feel how powerfully Lincoln used the rule of three in his Gettysburg Address, read this sentence aloud:

"But in a larger sense we cannot dedicate, we cannot consecrate, we cannot hallow this ground."

Consecrate and *hallow* express very nearly the same idea—for brevity's sake one could have been omitted. Try the shortened version out loud:

"But in a larger sense we cannot dedicate, we cannot hallow this ground."

With only two *cannots* the sentence falls flat, its rhythm and power gone. Add a fourth *cannot* and listen to how it sounds:

"But in a larger sense we cannot honor, we cannot dedicate, we cannot consecrate, we cannot hallow this ground."

Again the sentence lacks rhythm and its power is lost.

When you're listing people or concrete things, don't hesitate to use groups of two, four or whatever number is required. But when you're describing ideas, emotions and opportunities, your concept will always gain power by being expressed in three terms rather than two, four or a larger number.

Working a longer list down to three is easy—you simply compare the terms and discard the weakest one. Often on close study you'll realize that two of your terms mean very nearly the same thing. Cutting one of them adds punch.

Increasing two terms to three can be more difficult. Yet if you'll study what you want to say, you'll always be able to find a third term that adds to the depth and richness of your concept or description without being more than slightly redundant.

Here's how Harold J. Corbett, senior vice president of the Monsanto Company, used the rule of three in a speech to the Jaycees in Stillwater, Oklahoma. While discussing the general public's feelings about the chemical industry, he said:

> It finally dawned on us that we were a big part of the problem.
> We didn't understand the depth of their concerns.
> We didn't appreciate the intensity of their fear.
> And we didn't really believe how low we had sunk in the public's esteem—and how significant that is in the day-to-day operation of our business.
> Now we weren't alone. In many industries . . .

Mr. Corbett knew that *concerns* and *fear* are first cousins but he wanted to use *we didn't* three times for emphasis and rhythm. So he accepted this mild redundancy to gain the sweeping power of the rule of three.

The Majesty of Pairs

Addressing the Democratic National Convention in San Francisco, Jesse Jackson said:

There is a proper season for everything. There is a time to sow and a time to reap. There is a time to compete and a time to cooperate.

With those pairs Mr. Jackson lifted his statement to poetic heights in a moving speech.

Repetition

No speaker ever used a repetitious rhythm with greater impact than Winston Churchill. At a school he had attended as a young man, he spoke with particular brevity and simplicity:

"Never give in. Never give in. Never, never, never, never—in nothing, great or small, large or petty—never give in except to convictions of honor and good sense."

Defying Hitler, Churchill vowed in another speech:

"We shall fight on the beaches. We shall fight on the landing grounds. We shall fight in the fields and in the streets. We shall fight in the hills. We shall never surrender."

Initial Rhyme

With phrases like "nattering nabobs of negativism," Spiro Agnew proved that alliteration can be carried too far. But what can't be carried too far? As with every technique, initial rhyme must be used with restraint. Don't reach too far into *Roget*'s *Thesaurus*, as Spiro's sputtering speechwriter did. If you can't make the initial rhyme work with widely known words, forget it.

Round Off Large Numbers

Then use them in an illustrative way. It's more difficult for an audience to deal with numbers than with words. Statistics are not easily grasped, much less remembered. Yet the numbers you give must be readily comprehended by the majority of your audience; otherwise the resulting confusion will undermine your speech's effectiveness rather than contribute to it.

Use numbers to make a point by including a quickly understood reference, as Angier Biddle Duke's gem did in his speech before the Town Hall of Los Angeles:

> ... the size of a market depends on purchasing power more than on number of people. For example, the market for automobiles is about the same size in Denmark, with 5 million people, as it is in India, with 635 million people.

Is this kind of information available only to the members of the establishment? Hardly. It can be found in *The World Almanac*, available in any bookstore for about the price of a hamburger at the Hard Rock Cafe.

GIVE YOUR SPEECH THE POWER STROKE

Now let's talk less about style and more about power in speaking. The two are closely intertwined. But style won't, by itself, lift your speech out of mediocrity. Here's what will.

When You Stand Up, Let the Count Begin

Say what you mean. People didn't come to hear you hedge, apologize and pussyfoot around—they came to find out what you believe. Wear boots and spurs to the podium, not slippers.

Look at the following two paragraphs, both of which say the same thing:

> Permit me to hazard, not a prediction but a guess, about the possible future course of the economy. On balance, I believe that wholesale prices will tend to move onto somewhat higher ground over the course of the coming year.

> Next year wholesale prices will be higher.

The first statement is plain about only one thing: The speaker has no confidence in his convictions. Why then should the audience bother to listen to him? They can do as well spending their time wondering how he'd look with a mustache.

The second statement lets the audience know the speaker has the valor of his views. He could be wrong—they know predictions are risky—but they'll pay attention. They're forced to. Bold assertions are too compelling to ignore.

If you would be compelling, *say what you think in plain language*.

Use the Active Form

A speech in passive form can be cut twenty percent or more by converting it to the active form. Doing so adds punch and power. Consider these two examples:

Passive form: "The directive was received in our office the next day."

Active form: "Our office received the directive the next day."

Better yet: "We got the directive the next day."

The second active version is forty percent shorter than the passive form—that's a lot of shortening.

The active form can be overdone too. For a change of pace, drop back to the passive form about once in a dozen sentences. But keep more than ninety percent of your speech pulsing with the life that only the active form can give it.

Use Vigorous Words

Vigorous words aren't always short—*vigorous* is three syllables—but they're seldom longer than three. Usually they're just one sharp, direct syllable.

Flabby	*Vigorous*
facilitate	help
imperatives	needs
eventuated	happened, resulted
encourage	urge

Use Specific Words

They're great fog cutters. Every foggy word you speak will cause some of the audience to wander off your path.

Cut	*Replace With*
conveyance	carriage, deed, high-speed train
vehicle	car, truck, bicycle, medium, agent, ricksha
meal	snack, brunch, breakfast, quick bite

State Specific Ideas

During every presidential campaign all candidates are criticized for talking in generalities. They have an excuse —their audience numbers a quarter billion people. Your audience is smaller, which means you must get more specific. A lot more specific.

Use Bright Language

For example, *upchuck* has a recorded history going back to 1927 and is listed as standard usage by Webster (see Sources). *Upchuck* isn't slang; it isn't vulgar. Nor does it refer to a subject that's especially welcome after dinner, much less before. However, if you want to express dislike for a proposed course of action with this reference, *upchuck* is the better choice. Its Latin-derived equivalent is clinical, just as long when spoken, and no more palatable.

Don't Worry Much About Grammar

A speech is heard, not read. If your ideas are vigorous, if your words are bright and free of fog, and if your pace is brisk, they won't have time to bother about whether you should have said *as* instead of *like*.

Trust your ear for whether you should say *that* or *which*. (In case of doubt, say *that* and you're certain to be right.)

Who and *whom* is worth a moment to get right. It's strange that we have so much trouble with this distinction —we don't have any problem knowing whether to say *he* or *him*. That's the clue.

Take the sentence, "Who did what to whom?" You can substitute "She did that to him," but not "Him did that to she."

Who can be replaced by *he*, *she*, or *they*—no m's.

Whom can be replaced by *him*, *her*, *them*—the m-words.

One final thought on grammar. Beware of pointless rules. There are many. For example, some grammarians claim that a sentence should never end with a preposition.

"What are you looking at?" is wrong in their view. Apparently they'd prefer, "At what are you looking?" Winston Churchill responded to the grammarians on this question with, "This is the sort of English up with which I will not put."

Do likewise. If a sentence rings true to your ear, say it.

USE EXAMPLES TO POUND YOUR POINT HOME

Win Borden, president of the Minnesota Association of Commerce and Industry, in a speech to graduates of the St. Cloud State University:

> *Third, demand the best from yourself, because others will demand the best from you.*

Some years ago, Winston Lloyd, who later became one of America's top foreign policy experts, began his career as an aide to then Secretary of State Henry Kissinger. He presented the secretary with a long awaited report on conflicts in South America.

Without even glancing at the report, which Lloyd was holding out to him, Kissinger asked, "Is this the very best you can do?"

Lloyd stammered a bit, and said there were a few informational gaps.

"Take it back," was all that Kissinger said, and dismissed him.

Two weeks later, after working night and day, Lloyd again entered Kissinger's office and held out the report.

"Is this the very best you can do?" asked Kissinger without looking at the document.

Lloyd hesitated and admitted that some sections could be more complete. Kissinger angrily ordered him to take it back.

Three weeks later, Lloyd asked for another meeting. Again Kissinger asked, "Is this the very best you can do?"

And Lloyd replied, "Mr. Secretary, it's my best effort."

Kissinger smiled and said, "That's all I ever ask. I'll be happy to read your report."

The lesson here: Successful people don't simply give a project hard work. They give it their very best work.

Only one or two examples as long as the one above should be used. Mix them up with shorter ones, as Borden did in the same speech:

History is written by risk takers, most of whom were told, quite often, that they were crazy. For example, what do you think the reaction would have been had Ronald Reagan confided, during the filming of *Bedtime for Bonzo*, that he wanted to quit the movies and become President of the United States?

GRABBING THEM BY THE NUMBERS

If the senior partner in a firm, while speaking to some promising young executives, says, "I've been with this company a long time," it does not have a great impact. If however he says, "I joined this company when I was about the same age as many of you young men are today. Now

I'm sixty-two and near the end of the road with this company."

Now he's got them counting; he's got them thinking; he's got them, period. Each and every one of them knows he's been with the company for thirty-two years. Letting them figure it out had greater impact than simply giving the numbers.

You can overdo this. Avoid making your audience work too hard. But you do want them to participate with you in your speech.

I never scored better with this device than in the speech given in Chapter 10. At this writing the impact of the year 2000 has long since vanished—it's now far too familiar.

But I gave that speech in 1970 to a group of high school graduates and their parents. Thirty years was more than half again as long as those teenagers had lived—a vast span of time they found as difficult to imagine as I had at the same age.

So bringing the year 2000 into focus in relation to their lives grabbed their attention. It shocked them. At the podium I could feel the effect, and from then on I had them.

George Orwell achieved that same effect throughout the English-reading world when he published his most famous novel, *1984*, thirty-five years before the year he predicted would be so grim.

When it's appropriate to achieve this shock of time's swift flight, hit your audience with a vivid reminder that the world of thirty to thirty-five years from now is rushing at them.

QUOTATIONS

In putting the final polish on your speech, you may want to quote someone who reinforces your argument or paints it with eloquence from a different brush. Bookstores and libraries have books of quotations. Many are arranged by subject and cross-indexed by key words. (See the Sources appendix.)

You may find it worthwhile to keep a file of quotes that appeal to you. Index them by subject for quick reference. To be effective, a quotation must fit the topic of your remarks in a way that's immediately clear to the audience.

Since my speeches lean to the lighthearted, at the podium I'm more apt to quote the comedian than the scientist, poet or statesman. I've been known to recall some of the words of my special hero, the late, great W. C. Fields, who said:

"A woman drove me to drink—and I never had the courtesy to thank her."

Or I might quote Joe E. Lewis, who would sometimes use this routine:

"Ladies and gentlemen, in our audience tonight is a lovely lady. I'd like to introduce Miss Ellie Stillwell."

She'd stand up and there'd be a lot of applause. Then Lewis would say, "That's Ellie Stillwell, a girl who'll have a wonderful time tonight—if she'll only listen to reason."

Sometimes Lewis would say, "You can lead a horse to water—but if you can get him to roll over and float on his back you've got something."

Quotations must not only be relevant to your subject, your use of each one must also move your message forward. Of course if your subject is fun, any quote that gets a laugh keeps your message bubbling.

Once you have the body of your speech well in hand, it's time to get serious about finding a strong opening statement.

YOUR OPENING REMARKS

Make your beginning crisp and hard-hitting. George Jessel said, "If you haven't struck oil in your first two or three minutes, stop boring."

You have two goals to achieve with your opening remarks:

- to build rapport with the audience,
- and to tell them what your speech will be about.

Do this by relating yourself to the gathering, the location and the occasion.

But don't explain the obvious, the inconsequential or the unnecessary. Tell them what you're going to tell them in simple terms.

YOUR CLOSING REMARKS

Prepare your ending last, when you know exactly what you have to summarize or call a halt to. A strong speech has a powerful ending. If you're giving a lighthearted speech, leaving them laughing is the strongest finish you can make. Second best—but still good—is to end on an inspirational note.

An informational speech should conclude with a summary of the points made. If you want the audience to do something, sound the call to battle stations. Fire their imagination. If you've gotten them interested in your ideas, you should have them ready to move.

But never bring in new ideas at the conclusion. The place to do this is in the body of the speech.

Once you're satisfied that your speech contains essentially all you want to say, arranged the way you want to say it, you're ready to move into the rehearsal stage.

• •

Leave Out: jargon and references to inside information that some of the audience won't understand.
The people you shut out will retaliate by shutting you and your message out.

• •

CHAPTER 8

Rehearsing Your Speech

Rehearse to keep your speech moving at a brisk pace. In Will Rogers's words, "Even if you're on the right track, you'll get run over if you just stay there."

TRIAL RUN

Once you have your speech polished, your first move should be to find a willing victim to listen to it. Ideally, this audience of one person would be someone who is typical of the audience you will address. Usually, however, you'll have to settle for whomever you can get.

Deliver your speech from notes to your test audience of one and ask him to interrupt anytime he doesn't understand what you're saying or feels that you're making too obvious a point.

Consider your test audience's opinion carefully. However, remember that you are the final judge of what your real audience needs to be told and will understand.

GET YOURSELF VIDEOTAPED

The best rehearsal is to have yourself videotaped in a public-speaking class. Videotape is so valuable in acquiring delivery skills that any good public-speaking school today is sure to have this capability.

If you haven't seen yourself on videotape much, you'll be surprised to discover that everybody in the class looks like themselves on tape. *Except you.* Our self-images are rarely mirror images.

When you view your first taped speech to the class, you'll see that you don't look as nervous as you felt. And you'll probably see a few things you should avoid doing. For example, some beginning speakers will unaccountably come up with new mannerisms when giving a talk to a group. This might be standing with one shoulder held high or nervously pulling at their clothing. For catching these twitches, nothing touches the videotape.

But the most important function of videotape is building confidence. Specifically, it will make you see that your nervousness *doesn't show like you thought it did.*

DO-IT-YOURSELF VIDEO

If you can't make it to a public-speaking class, the next best thing is to do it yourself. Rent a videotape camera if you don't own or have access to one. Look in the yellow pages under video rentals.

If you have to do this alone, set the video camera on a tripod and, using a long cable, control the camera yourself while you're speaking. Or just focus on your make-do podium, start the camera, walk into the picture and start talking.

TIMING YOUR RATE OF SPEECH

Use a cassette recorder to concentrate your attention on sounds, not sights. Take a newspaper or magazine, mark a starting place, and read for one minute in your best speaking voice at your natural, comfortable speed.

Count the words and you'll know your ordinary pace. Count the long and short words alike—they'll balance out.

If you speak at about 150 words a minute, fine. You've passed the test and can go on to other things.

However, if your natural pace is less than 125 or more than 175 words a minute, be on your guard.

If you talk too slowly, the audience's attention will wander and you'll lose them.

On the other hand, if you speak considerably more rapidly than the normal 150 words, a large part of the audience may not even try to follow you. Only a few public speakers choose to speak rapidly, on the theory that doing so forces the audience to pay close attention. To get away with this, the speaker's enunciation must be exceptional. Unless yours is, rehearse (with material other than your speech) until you feel comfortable talking at 175 words a minute or less.

How do you rehearse to speed up or slow down your speech?

Take a book you'll enjoy using for this purpose and count 150 words in it. Then measure the length that that many words occupy on the page. Type and page sizes vary, but 150 words will probably measure about 2½ inches. Once you've determined that distance accurately for your book, you can take a ruler and quickly mark off a number of sections of about 150 words.

Every morning and evening, pick up that book and read one passage for exactly one minute. Within a few days you'll be hitting the end of the passage right on the button —or certainly close enough.

BREATHING

How you sound depends on how you breathe and control your air supply. In breathing for life, inhalation and exhalation consume about the same amount of time. In breathing for speech, the pattern changes to quick inhalations between phrases, taking no more than one sixth of the usual time, followed by slow and irregular exhalations as we talk.

Untrained speakers tend to breathe lightly, using only their upper chests. Trained speakers are more likely to draw air deeply into their lungs and control it with their abdominal muscles. Learning to breathe deeply and to control the flow of air with your abdominal muscles should be practiced at first for only a breath or two to avoid hyper-ventilating.

Practice taking the deepest breath you can and then talking loudly the instant your lungs are full. Keep talking as long as you can without taking another breath.

Until you can control the flow of air from your lungs with your abdominal muscles, you can't achieve the fullest and most resonant tone that you're capable of.

VOICE

If you're dissatisfied with how your voice sounds or with your diction, college courses or private instruction offer the best environment for quick improvement.

You may not wish to wait for the next semester to start. Considerable commuting time, tuition expense and inconvenience may be involved in either classroom or private instruction. In such cases a practical alternative is self-instruction. You can make rapid progress with a tape recorder and a copy of *Training the Speaking Voice* (see Sources). You'll do even better working with a friend who shares your interest.

GESTURES AND FACIAL EXPRESSIONS

Practice your gestures and such things as emphasizing a point with a raised eyebrow before a mirror. However, if you plan to make extensive use of the nonverbal acting skills, take yourself to a drama class. This is not your highest priority in public speaking, however—beyond the first few rows, facial expressions aren't seen well except when a spotlight is used. Generally it's enough to smile at appropriate moments; the rest of the time a relaxed but alert expression is best.

No gestures at all are better than too many. You don't want to look like you're doing your t'ai chi ch'uan exercises in quick time. Better they should concentrate on your words, even at the cost of perhaps one in ten of the audience thinking you stand a little rigidly.

HOW MUCH REHEARSAL DO I NEED?

Only you really know. You should rehearse until you feel you have it. Not memorized word for word, but well in mind so that you can talk forcefully from your notes.

To reach that point, run through your speech at least twice but no more than ten times. That's a wide range. How many times depends more on how afraid you are of stage fright than on any other element. Feeling that you're overprepared will give you a lot of extra confidence.

The speech can get a little hackneyed in your mind because you know it so well that you become a little disinterested. That's a danger. You can get so used to your speech that it sounds like you've gone over it a hundred times. The crowd can sense this.

If you're really nervous about getting up before a large crowd—perhaps for your first time except for practice sessions—it's less likely that you'll sound stale. In this case keep rehearsing until it feels right, but don't go over ten repetitions.

If you're confident, you'll start losing ground to staleness if you go beyond three repetitions. You probably won't notice it—the signs are subtle—but the edge will start coming off your delivery.

Save some excitement for the actual speech. I lean toward underpreparing, but I realize that I'm basing that on long experience. It doesn't matter much if you miss delivering some of the fine phrases you polished into your speech. What counts is getting the essence across.

I've heard a lot of people get tangled up in their words before saying, "What I mean is . . .," and what comes out next is better than what they'd written. It happens because they were right on the subject matter; they were getting feedback from the audience; and they were determined to get their thought across. Feel that way and you can't go wrong.

I'm certain that audiences share my feelings. I'd rather see someone grope for words occasionally than get up and run through a speech by rote in a monotonous singsong.

PREPARING FOR THE QUESTION-AND-ANSWER PERIOD

Question-and-answer periods often are fun. They're certainly great exercises in thinking fast on your feet.

But the Q and A can be no fun at all when you're obliged to defend positions, actions or inactions that are unpopular with all or part of the audience. If you like getting banged around, go into such a session unprepared.

Anticipation is the best protection. When you sit down to list the questions you might get, pay close attention to where your armor is thin. That's where a hostile audience will hit you.

Have your file of questions handy while you work on your speech so you can add any that occur to you. Don't stop there. We all have unique viewpoints and our own special blind spots.

Explain your topic to your friends, preferably to individuals who have something in common with the expected audience. Ask those friends what questions they might raise themselves. Also ask what questions they can imagine other people, especially hostile people, raising.

Then prepare answers for all the anticipated questions. Keep in mind that your answer can be straight or witty.

Straight answers are required when you're asked honest questions seeking information of wide interest. When the question involves something the audience is reasonably concerned about, preface your answer with a statement of your awareness of and sympathy for their concerns.

But questioners sometimes take a long-winded trip down Ego Lane. Watch the crowd during a tiresomely drawn out dissertation from the floor. If the questioner seems to be expressing the audience's feelings, give a detailed answer that sticks to the facts as you know them. However, if a polysyllabic show-off makes the audience restless with digressions or circumlocutions, answer with something like, "Beats the hell out of me. Next question, please."

Orben's *Current Comedy* (see Sources) and his books often suggest ways to handle difficult or hostile interrogators. As a response to a long, rapid-fire question, Bob Orben suggests: "Well, in answer to the questioner with the aerobic tongue, let me just say..."

REPEAT THE QUESTION

Even in a small meeting room, the people sitting behind the questioner usually can't hear the question, so they miss the point of your reply. This makes them restless. Avoid this by always repeating each question over the mike before answering it.

Repeating the question helps you in two ways. First, it keeps the communication flowing and the entire audience involved. Second, it digs a trap for the complicated quizzers. While a long-winded bore is going on and on, the rest of the audience is suffering with you. They don't want you to repeat the questioner's harangue, so they'll support whatever way you choose to shorten it.

Q AND A OPPORTUNITIES

The Q and A is a splendid opportunity to fire off an occasional one-liner and get some laughs, but be careful to keep it in good fun. You can win the audience with a strong speech and then lose them with sarcastic replies to legitimate questions.

Some speakers plant supporters in the audience to ask the questions they most want to answer. To my mind this steps over the line between ethical persuasion and unethical manipulation.

There's a way to accomplish the same object without playing tricks on the audience. Here's how:

Put each question you'd like to answer on a card. Then, toward the end of the Q and A—or after responding to a difficult or embarrassing question—tell the audience:

"There's a question I've been hoping someone would ask me—and after that last one I think I deserve a chance to try to balance things out. Here we go. What if . . .?"

And now you raise a possibility that's highly favorable to your cause. Not only is the question you aim at yourself positive, your answer can be even more so. This can be an effective way to introduce ideas that are a little too challenging or speculative to be included in the body of your remarks.

Don't repeat yourself. Use this technique to bring out different points or new theories not raised by your speech. And you can simply say, "Audiences often ask me, what happens if . . ."

• •

Leave Out: sounds like, "Ah, uh, um."
Just pause as you grope for words.

• •

Leave Out: "Now if you will just give me a few more minutes . . ." Apologizing for talking too long adds insult to injury.

Chapter 9

Delivering Your Speech

The countdown starts two weeks before the event, when your speech is outlined, polished and well-rehearsed.

At this time call the program chairperson and check on possible last-minute changes in the event's schedule. Double-check your travel arrangements and confirm that someone will meet you, if that was the agreement.

Read and watch the news now with a special eye for late-breaking developments you can play on in your talk. Now that you know your speech well, you're likely to find pertinent items in the news jumping out at you. Dropping a few of these gems into your remarks adds a powerful sense of immediacy that you can get in no other way.

When you call two weeks before the event, pin down who will introduce you. If possible, meet your introducer —at least by phone—at this time.

As I've said before, don't leave the important element of introduction to chance. You can't stand at the podium listing your accomplishments without sounding like a braggart, so go to whatever trouble it takes to have a reliable person introduce you to the audience. That person can detail your triumphs in a way that establishes your credentials while you make modest faces.

Tom Dewey was the man everybody thought would take the presidency from Truman—everybody but Truman himself. Dewey often went to the mike without a glance at what his speechwriters had put in his hand. Whether or not that habit cost him the election, on one occasion during the campaign he was mortified by it. After reading a couple of pages to a large audience with his customary vigor, it dawned on him that he was extolling his own virtues in terms so direct the audience was embarrassed for him. Dewey then realized he was making the remarks his speechwriters had intended for his introducer. Dewey's speechwriters had the right idea, their man just didn't have the right page.

PSYCH-UP

Shortly before you get up to make your remarks is the time to visualize yourself delivering a confident, well-received speech. It works—if you've done your homework well and have earned the right to psych yourself up.

Think of times you've succeeded at your endeavors in any field rather than the times you've failed. Think in terms of how good it'll be to succeed rather than how bad it'll be to fail. Think about your purpose in delivering the speech.

Concentrate on what you want to do. Concentrate on the emotions you want to spread outward, not on the emotions you want to keep inside. Concentrate on what you're saying, not how you're saying it or how you look.

Once we've learned how to do something, our ability to do it well often depends on the degree of our concentration. Those who really achieve have the ability to focus intensely on their goal and, while they're performing, keep a lid on their negative emotions.

Psych-up is important. But you're setting yourself up for disaster if you rely on psych-up to take the place of preparation. If you suddenly have to land an airplane by yourself, unless you know how to fly you'll experience tension to the same painful degree that characterizes advanced stage fright.

If you're reading this chapter first in hopes of finding a shortcut around putting the time into creating, revising and rehearsing your speech, forget it. Expert speakers make it look easy, just as expert ice skaters or jugglers make what they've spent years practicing look easy.

Many people won't step onto a dance floor until several other couples are out there. This is stage fright—the reluctance to separate yourself from an anonymous group and become someone others can watch perform.

Without preparation all of us can argue a point we feel deeply about with great conviction on a one-to-one basis. Why then can't we simply stand up before a thousand people and argue that same point just as effectively and without preparation?

Because we have been arguing with conviction on a one-to-one basis since early childhood. We *know* we can do it—a lifetime of experience eliminates all doubt.

Speaking before an audience is a performance. Doing it

well requires four things: preparation, at least a minimum level of performing skill, belief in the worth of your message, and confidence in your ability to deliver it.

However, your goal in preparing a speech should not be to attain complete relaxation at the podium. You don't want to relax up there, you want to perform well. To do that you need to gear yourself to your highest level of performance.

Controlled stage fright is the key to high performance, first because it drives you to prepare adequately, second because immediately before you begin to speak, it raises your concentration and energy to a high level.

In Chapter 1 we talked about stage fright as something that happens at some time in the future. Now we're looking at the moment when you stand up to speak—perhaps for the first time before a crowd as large or important to you. So a few more hints about stage fright are in order here.

Those who speak frequently in public rarely or never feel the most acute symptoms of stage fright—as long as they continue doing what they're trained for and used to doing. However, getting involved in new areas of public performance can bring on acute stage fright again.

Some actors have always spoken lines other people have written until suddenly on live TV they have to speak for themselves. Many of them find it a terrifying experience—because they're not prepared.

After being on TV and speaking to crowds in many situations for years, I decided to develop my own headline act for Las Vegas. Did I feel an unpleasant amount of stage fright the first time I stepped out on a Las Vegas stage? You bet I did. But long experience enabled me to convert that negative feeling into a positive rush of energy. As soon as I was into my act the stage fright vanished, leaving only intense energy behind.

However, I didn't just wander out on stage one night. I developed my act over a period of time, tried bits of its material out on banquet audiences, and booked myself into small clubs around the country to perfect the material. Not until I had perfected my performance did I appear in Las Vegas.

TAKE A MINUTE BEFORE YOU BEGIN

There's no hurry when you reach the podium; it's better not to start talking instantly. Give yourself a moment to catch your breath and get ready. Let the audience settle down. Let the noise subside.

Calm yourself. Get set to go. Like a golfer before the swing, take a lot of time. As the noise goes down in the hall, let that also happen inside your mind and body.

Look at the audience while you're getting set. Establish eye contact to left, center and right. Tell yourself they're just people out there, the same sort of people you talk to every day of the year. When you demonstrate confidence by looking them in the eye, you'll feel confidence rise inside you.

Then take a deep breath and begin.

EXCESSIVE TERSENESS

Terseness can be carried too far. At a company banquet in Denver the last speaker before me had just been introduced. I leaned back to enjoy his talk.

He said, "Brevity is the soul of wit," and sat down.

After a shocked silence the audience realized he really

had given his whole speech. Nervous titters swept the crowd. Somewhat lamely, the master of ceremonies introduced me. I took the mike and said, "Brevity is the sole of wit all right—but my arches have fallen."

The crowd roared because they had been embarrassed *for* the other speaker. Now they decided his six-word speech had been a setup for me. At such times almost any good-hearted ad-lib will get a laugh—one that'll launch your speech beautifully.

However, there are situations where extreme brevity is the best policy. I saw this one time when Danny Thomas made a very impassioned speech. He not only covered everything that needed to be said on that occasion, he had the audience convulsed with laughter one moment and crying the next. Danny finished to a tremendous ovation and started walking out of the hall.

Now it was Joey Bishop's turn to speak. When Joey reached the mike he told the audience, "Whatever he said goes for me *double*," and then he ran after Danny.

When the previous speaker not only can't be topped—he can't be approached—don't even try. Cut and run.

"TURN AROUND AND LOOK AT ME"

At most banquets, people sit at round tables, which means many of them have their backs to the head table and others are at angles to you.

If that's the situation when I reach the mike, I always say, "Before we begin, I know that some of you have had a lovely chance to visit at your table, but now everything that's going to happen for the rest of the night is going to take place right up here. If you're not facing this way, that makes you uncomfortable. It makes me very uncomfortable talking to the back of your neck, so take a minute and turn your chair so you're facing this way."

If it's noisy, wait until things quiet down and then repeat your request. Give the audience time. Some of them might not have much space, but within a few moments they'll all get themselves turned around. When you've accomplished that you've just had a thousand or five hundred people do something for you. You haven't done a thing for them but they've done something for you—they've turned their chairs around. So all of a sudden you have a little hold on them. There's a little string attached to them from you. When you've tied that string you start with your speech. It's better because they're looking at you. They're more comfortable—they don't have cricks in their necks from turning around. They'll spend more time looking at you since it's not bothering them.

And you've done something else important—you've demonstrated control and confidence. That reassures the audience without them realizing it.

CARRYING ON AFTER A BLOOPER

If it's a very small one, just keep going. The odds are most of the audience won't notice or remember. If it's too big a blooper to ignore, enjoy it. That's the key. Refuse to be embarrassed. If you think of an ad-lib, let it fly. Laugh or grin sheepishly, whatever comes naturally, and get on with your speech. It's no big thing.

SPACE OUT AWARD-GIVING

I've often spoken at company dinners where they have a lot of awards to hand out. Usually they plan to get the awards over with all at once. When you do that, there are lots of people milling around and it seems to take forever. It's boring and the crowd gets restless.

If you're emceeing such an event, take control and slip the awards in one at a time, beginning with the smallest one and working up to the most important, to be given late in the program. Call one person up for an award and, while he's making his way to the front, have something else going on. Ideally, you'd have announcements and short speeches to mix in with the award-giving. If not, tell a joke, recognize someone who won't be coming forward, or fire off a one-liner to occupy the time.

Plan these things ahead so you can avoid dead mike time. Either you control an audience or they control you. Unless you keep something interesting going on at the podium, the crowd will be chattering at their tables, and, when you're finally ready to have something happen, you can't make yourself heard.

VARY YOUR DELIVERY

Some monotonous speakers resort to pounding the gavel to quiet chatterers. One particularly boring speaker once swung the gavel so hard he broke it. The mallet flew off, striking a man in the front row on the head. When the speaker apologized, the injured listener cried out, "Hit me again—I can still hear you."

Your purpose in standing before the audience may be to inform and persuade them, to entertain them, or to discharge a ceremonial function. Unless you want to convince your listeners to avoid you and your ideas in the future, inflicting monotony on them will destroy your message.

How is monotony avoided?

By putting variety in its place. Vary the speed with which you speak, vary your tone and volume, vary the length of your sentences.

Ask a question now and then. With small groups, it's often effective to make a point of getting an answer from someone in the audience before continuing.

Break up a series of long, involved ideas with a short, punchy sentence now and then. The short sentences can consist of as few as three words, subject, verb and object, as in "We need trees."

Use graphic contrasts: "In America we shorten our lives eating too much; in the Third World millions starve."

Use the names of some of the people in the audience. You don't have to know the individuals personally to do this. I didn't know all the teenagers in the speech given in Chapter 10. And, in many of my after-dinner talks before and since then, I've mentioned people in the audience whom I've met only briefly or not at all. It's always effective. People love it—not just the individuals who are singled out—everyone in the audience loves it. Recognizing or praising individuals in a group extends recognition and praise to the entire group. It shows you know more about them than they thought you did. And that is something every audience likes to hear.

HOW TO BRING THINGS TO A SUCCESSFUL CONCLUSION

Lord Mancroft said, "You can't tell whether a man is a finished speaker until he finishes speaking." Don't run down to an apology, run up to a climax. Then close your mouth. You're through. Sit down and enjoy the rest of the evening.

• •

Leave Out: "Thank you very much."
Make your final statement, pause or nod, and step back. If you're tempted to close with thanks, imagine Patrick Henry proclaiming, "Give me liberty or give me death. Thank you very much."

• •

> *"Be sincere. Be brief. Be seated."*
> —Franklin Delano Roosevelt

CHAPTER 10

A Speech I'm Proud Of

Most of the hundreds of after-dinner talks I've given are like kisses in the dark; only memories remain. Happily, a transcript has survived of a speech I've always considered among my best.

It was the commencement address delivered at the Bronxville High School in Bronxville, New York, on June 20, 1970. My son, Mike, was in the graduating class.

I considered it quite an honor. I had given a lot of speeches by then, though not nearly as many as I've given since. But this one, for Mike and his friends in the graduating class, was special. I didn't want to embarrass him.

It was an exclusive area and many prominent families lived there. Being Ed McMahon hardly was going to impress those kids much.

It didn't even impress my kids much; they were used to

my being on television. I recall a conversation when my children were quite young. A friend said, "My daddy goes to the bank every day." My kid said, "My daddy goes to the television show every day," as if I went to see the show.

So I had to give a good speech. I didn't want to lecture them because I was, after all, just another parent. Also, it was a time when the discord and tragedy of the Vietnam War was wracking the country. Young people were rebellious and regarded anyone above the age of thirty as suspect. I was definitely over thirty.

For weeks I scribbled notes on the backs of ticket envelopes and scraps of paper as I traveled about. I wanted this to be as good as I could make it.

I'm not a saver. I don't have a lot of copies of past speeches, but I have this speech because the full text was printed in the local paper, the Bronxville *Review Press-Reporter*.

It was very much a speech of its time, as speeches should be. Its allusions were designed for the moment, and the meaning of some vanished with the month. But the speech accomplished its purpose, which is as apparent now as it was then.

It's nice to be in Bronxville. In this day and age it's nice to be anyplace. And it's especially nice to work for a group of people that are not in their pajamas.

I would like to properly introduce myself. In these quarters I'm known as Mike McMahon's father. I can't overemphasize that and I don't mean to be facetious, but oftentimes when you move into a new area your doorway to the community is opened by your children.

Mike's success on the football field has made me known around here, and that's nice. When you work in television or in the public eye it can become tiresome always being "on stage" and I think it is important for your psyche to keep in proper focus what you really are. It's so easy to get carried away with yourself and let your so-called importance get blown out of proportion.

But it seems whenever you start thinking you're a big deal something always happens to bring you right down to earth. Like the time I was walking along Park Avenue and had to get a check cashed at a branch of a bank where I was not well known. All along the way while I was walking down the street I could hear people say, "That's him. That looks like Ed McMahon. That's him. He's a lot taller when you see him in person. Gee, he's a lot thinner than he is on television, but that's him. That looks like Ed McMahon. Yes that's definitely him."

Well, you get to feel a little important. You think you're kind of special. You have to feel that way, any human being would, and as I turned in the bank I heard somebody say, "That's definitely Ed McMahon." I walked up to the teller and he said, "Do you have any identification?"

And worse than that—the time that Johnny and I were having lunch in Sardi's. It was on a Wednesday. A couple of typical matinee ladies—with the funny hats and the little flowers—were sitting opposite us. We could hear one say, "No, no, you go. You ask them." And the other one would say, "No, no. You ask them." This went on for some time, and John and I got to feeling kind of funny. Finally one of them walked over —we were feeling pretty good at this point—and she said, "If you're not going to use the cream, can we have it?"

So tonight it's nice to be Mike McMahon's father, and I'm truly thrilled and honored to be speaking at his and your commencement.

So thank you Dr. Braun, distinguished guests, parents, brothers and sisters and people that have no other place to go on a warm Saturday night—and graduates. That sounds pretty tough, doesn't it?

Graudates. I can still remember my night. Just thirty years ago tonight, almost to the very day, Saturday, June 22, at the Memorial Auditorium in Lowell, Massachusetts.

I sat there like you're sitting tonight wondering about myself. What was I going to do? Who was I? Where was I headed? Well, as a matter of fact, it wasn't all that serene. To be truthful, I almost missed my own graduation.

Let me tell you the story. I was so anxious to get working in my field of announcing that I took a job working on a sound truck, the kind of truck that travels around the countryside announcing the great features of a political candidate, the coming of a fair or some development that would be of interest to the community.

I was the announcer in the back and I did this for several nights before my graduation and missed all the rehearsals. But I had a friend by the name of Lawrence McMahon, and I told him to save a seat for me next to him and I'd make the graduation. Well, as it turned out, we were late coming into the city (the truck got tied up in traffic) and finally I arrived just as the headmaster, Ray Sullivan, was making his main address. Now all of the graduates were behind him in a choir loft that went up right to the top of the auditorium. That was behind the main speaker and out front were three thousand people in the auditorium.

Now I snuck in the back and tried to sneak to my seat. As I came in I was still putting on my cap and gown and I got down, just about to my row, and the laughter was finally so loud from the audience that the headmaster, Ray Sullivan (and he was not the kind of guy you would take to right away. In fact it took me until graduating night and I still wasn't sure), interrupted his speech to look around and see what all the commotion was. And there I was sneaking into my seat. All I knew to do was just give him a big wave and say, "Hi, Ray."

So let me double-check and make sure everybody is

here. Is Joan Brennan here? How about John Reetz and Tia Doyle? Is Steve Pass here? And Rob Leary, Tim Collins? How about Dew-Ga-Lew, Lou Gobble?

And Marcie Carleton, Steve Pitman and Cutch? How about Kevin Coughlan? And did Rudy Toast and Mike make it? What about Ray-Da-Bay-Say-Hay! Okay, then we can begin.

Thirty years ago, my graduation, such a long time and yet not so long ago. They say that none of the young trust anyone over thirty, and I compound that consequence by telling you that it was thirty years ago when I graduated from high school. Long ago? Consider this. When your sons and daughters graduate thirty years from now it will be the year 2000. That's a little heavy, isn't it? The year 2000.

So let's right away start talking straight to one another. All the bull about the generation gap. Let's put it where it is. There was a past. There's a present. There'll be a future. Where does everybody here tonight fit in? Well, let me tell you as a parent and part of the past, that a lot of us over-twenties here tonight are distressed, uptight.

Where did we fail? How did we let you down? That bewilderment promotes, "You just don't understand, Mom. Dad, it's not like that anymore." (I'm sure you parents have heard remarks like these.)

To be a little facetious, it's my personal opinion that the generation gap started with the new math—and one other thing—and I'm serious now, the sorcerer. We gave you to the sorcerer. From the time you were able to sit up the sorcerer would take you for three or four hours a day and tell you wonderful stories, spin beautiful dreams, play enchanting music. He made you laugh, taught you to sing and always suggested good things to eat.

He told you of wonderful toys you could buy. A few hours every day of every year, the sorcerer took you to a wonderful world of music, laughter, adventure and incredible goings-on. And in glaring contrast to your parents and teachers, the sorcerer never scolded you. He never told you to go to bed early or do your homework. The sorcerer only brought pleasure. The sorcerer, television. It's estimated by the head of the Federal Communications Commission that by the time a young person enters first grade, he has spent more hours watching television than he will spend in a college classroom. We didn't lose you, we gave you away.

And here you are. One hundred and fourteen of the sorcerer's offspring, another crop of television babies fully grown, weaned on the tube. You've already learned more, eyewitnessed more in your eighteen years—far more than we ever did in ours.

Now we needn't spend too much time on the past here tonight. It had its hang-ups and its achievements. We saw leaders killed, stores looted and obscenities glorified. But we managed to conquer polio, transplant hearts, walk on the moon, and, no small miracle—Tiny Tim got married! And incidentally, if you saw our show that night, you were part of the largest audience we have ever had. That night our show matched the audience of the Super Bowl. Amazing! That many people to watch Tiny Tim get married. We almost didn't have a show that night. At first, the wedding was going to take place on *Mission: Impossible*!

But in a way I think it's good that Tiny Tim got married. Otherwise, he would have gone through life being known as just another pretty face!

Did you hear about the gown? You ladies will like this. It was eighteenth-century lace with a long train, and it was covered with silver sequins and star sapphires. And what the bride wore was sensational too.

So, let's press on to the present. I know the average high school graduating class isn't too keen on quotations, but let me give you two:

"There is even now something of ill omen amongst us. I mean the increasing disregard for law which pervades the country; the growing disposition to substitute the wild and furious passions, for the sober judgment of courts." That's Abraham Lincoln, January 27, 1838.

Here's another: "Our youth now loves luxury. They have bad manners, contempt for authority, disrespect for older people. Children nowadays are tyrants. They no longer rise when their elders enter the room. They contradict their parents, chatter before company, gobble their food and tyrannize their teachers." Sound familiar, current, like you heard it yesterday? That's Socrates, fourth century B.C. Well, the beat goes on.

A young girl named Allison Krause sticks a daisy into the gun barrel of a frightened National Guardsman and the next day he shoots her dead.

Three weeks ago, fifty young people with flowers and black-and-white arm bands cap off the Memorial Day parade here in Bronxville. People at a cocktail party later ask me, "What were those people trying to do? What did they mean?"

The present confrontation and the gap grow wider. A medical student raises his hand with the peace sign and he's clobbered by a hard hat. We see this confrontation everywhere. It seems that everybody's against everybody. Now there has to be a germ of hope in confrontation, some good. At least people are standing for something, standing up to be counted. But it has to be peaceful confrontation.

The right to dissent cannot be confused with the rage to destroy. Disagree doesn't mean disrupt and the flag can't be used to make a shirt nor become the symbol of only one side of the disagreement. And Socrates said something else that pertains to our times: "Violence is the retreat of the incompetent."

A moment ago I mentioned the word hope, and hope has always been the doorway to the future. So how bad is it even now?

We are the first nation to share our wealth. We valiantly fight for the right to have all voices heard, for the right of dissent and to disagree. And we strive to right the wrongs of the past. We made mistakes, of course, and you will too, that I can promise. But if time teaches, then at least don't you make the same mistakes. And if there has to be a generation gap, then what about a generation alliance? Take the best of what we are and add to it the best of what you can become. Remember, what is meaningful maintains. What is filled with promise proceeds on, and you young people are the untapped resource of this renaissance. And listen, don't throw things away just because we liked them. Don't discard them because we delighted so in them.

I promise you that you, too, will look back with extra regard for Miss Guinee's mouse, Tilu, extra feeling for Pete's and Fay's and extra love for the lot. So, from this rubble of destruction and debris I see hope. What is truly right remains and can be the great launching pad for all your ideas. Do you remember Senator Kennedy's favorite quotation? "Some men see things as they are and say, Why? I dream of things that never were and say, Why not?"

Do you want to get excited about your part in this? Do you want to get turned on to tomorrow? Well then, consider this. Since the dawn of time, man has been fighting to find his identity, to prove himself to be an individual. We find the young of the so-called hippie group and drug culture saying, "Let me be. I'm doing my own thing; I'm finding myself."

William Faulkner said this in 1950: "I believe that man will not merely endure. He will prevail. He is immortal not because he alone among creatures has an inexhaustible voice, but because he has a soul, a spirit capable of compassion and sacrifice and endurance." Wouldn't you say that Faulkner was together?

The dignity of man. What a concept. Man counts. The same man that throws the Budweiser can off the back of the boat can pick up a Milky Way wrapper and toss it in a litter can. The same man that shoots a pheasant for dinner can demonstrate to preserve the seals on Pribilof Island. The same man that throws a rock through a dean's widow can start a small businessman's instruction program for deprived citizens. They count. You count.

But the shoring up of tomorrow is not going to be especially easy. You won't be tiptoeing through any tulips! But there is a chance, and that's what hope is really all about, isn't it? And let's not leave us out. We count too. Us tottering old-timers who manage to make the 8:05 each day to the city and grind out eight to ten hours' worth of margin calls, meeting competitors' prices and production deadlines. We count, so think about us too, once in a while.

And think about the night when you'll be sitting out there in the audience in the year 2000 wondering when the commencement speaker is going to finish so that we can all get to the party afterward.

Think about this. Communication is a two-way street and we don't know much more about being the parents of eighteen-year-olds than you know about being eighteen years old. A generation alliance is a nice idea, isn't it? Like the Youngbloods sing on their big hit: "Come on people now, smile on your brother, everybody get together, gotta love one another right now!"

So tonight, young people, it's all yours. And thank God, high school's over. It's yours, Randy Shaw and Dwight Muckley and Katie Bennett and Pia Bogh and John Donohue, Barbara Heaphy, Jeanette Bartlette, Jenny Bond. Yours!

So, let me close with what has become the battle cry of the disadvantaged, and what I prefer to call a progress cry for all of us, for I believe it is filled with hope for all of our futures. "Right on, gang, right on!"

Reader, I say the same to you—your interest in public speaking is right on. The more you put into improving your oratorical skills, the more you'll gain in satisfaction, influence and opportunity.

SOURCES

Comedy Newsletter

Orben's Current Comedy. Published twice a month by The Comedy Center, 700 Orange Street, Wilmington, DE 19801. This newsletter is a must for anyone wanting to use humor in speeches.

Joke Books

McKENSIE, E. C. *14,000 Quips & Quotes for Writers and Speakers*. New York: Greenwich House, 1983. Arranged by subject. 581 pages.

ORBEN, ROBERT. *2400 Jokes to Brighten Your Speeches*. Garden City, New York: Doubleday & Company, Inc., 1984. Arranged by subject. 222 pages.

_____. *2100 Laughs for All Occasions*. Garden City, New

York: Doubleday & Company, Inc., 1983. Arranged by subject. 240 pages.

———. *2500 Jokes to Start 'Em Laughing*. Garden City, New York: Doubleday & Company, Inc., 1979. Arranged by subject. 226 pages.

———. *The Encyclopedia of One-Liner Comedy*. Garden City, New York: Doubleday & Company, Inc., 1971. Arranged by subject. 232 pages.

Inspiration

OTT, JOHN. *How to Write and Deliver a Spech*. New York: Trident Press, 1970. "The Ten-Minute Ordeal of George Morris" in Part III is an informative and inspiring fictional account of how a speech was prepared and what its successful delivery did for the speaker.

Speeches

Vital Speeches of the Day. Twice a month from City News Publishing Co., Box 606, Southold, NY 11971. On file in public, college and high school libraries throughout the United States. Indexed annually in the November 15 issue. Published since 1934. Available on microfilm.

Quotations

BARTLETT, JOHN. *Familiar Quotations*. Boston: Little, Brown and Company; fifteenth edition, 1980. Arranged chronologically by author; key word and phrase index. 1,540 pages.

PARTNOW, ELAINE. *The Quotable Woman, 1800–1981*. New York: Facts on File Publications, 1982. "Nearly 9,000 quotations . . . arranged chronologically according to the contributor's birthdate." 602 pages.

_____. *The Quotable Woman from Eve to 1799*. New York: Facts on File Publications, 1985. More than 6,000 quotations. 533 pages.

SELDES, GEORGE. *The Great Thoughts*. New York: Ballantine Books, 1985. An astounding collection of powerful ideas. 487 pages.

TRIPP, RHODA THOMAS. *International Thesaurus of Quotations*. New York: Thomas Y. Crowell, 1970. Arranged alphabetically by subject with cross-references. Key word and phrase index. Author and source index. 1,058 pages.

Other Reference Works for the Public Speaker

Webster's Ninth New Collegiate Dictionary. Springfield, Massachusetts: Merriam-Webster, Inc., 1985. Allows you to use words with confidence you might otherwise think were too slangy. 1,560 pages.

Roget's International Thesaurus. New York: Thomas Y. Crowell; Harper & Row; fourth edition, 1977. About 250,000 words arranged by meaning in 1,000 categories, most of which are separated into a dozen or more shades of meaning. Water travel, for example, has seventy-eight subdivisions. However, many searches for synonyms are quickly answered by checking the extensive alphabetical index. 1,317 pages.

Research

HOROWITZ, LOIS. *Knowing Where to Look: The Ultimate Guide to Research*. Cincinnati: Writer's Digest Books, 1984. 436 pages. Comprehensive and readable.

Voice

ANDERSON, VIRGIL A. *Training the Speaking Voice*. New York: Oxford University Press, 1977. Third edition. 461 pages. Bibliography.